European Works Councils in the Netherlands

European Works Councils in the Netherlands

Jan Cremers

This book was originally published as a monograph in the International Encyclopaedia of Laws/Labour Law and Industrial Relations.

Founding Editor: Roger Blanpain
General Editor: Frank Hendrickx
Volume Editor: Frank Hendrickx

Wolters Kluwer

Published by:
Kluwer Law International B.V.
PO Box 316
2400 AH Alphen aan den Rijn
The Netherlands
E-mail: lrs-sales@wolterskluwer.com
Website: www.wolterskluwer.com/en/solutions/kluwerlawinternational

Sold and distributed by:
Wolters Kluwer Legal & Regulatory U.S.
7201 McKinney Circle
Frederick, MD 21704
United States of America
Email: customer.service@wolterskluwer.com

ISBN 978-94-035-4690-2

e-Book: ISBN 978-94-035-4700-8
web-PDF: ISBN 978-94-035-4710-7

The Author

Jan Cremers is associated with the Law School of Tilburg. He acted as a European trade union leader and was a member of the European Parliament. In 2013, he received an honorary Doctor of Letters at the Westminster University 'in recognition of his services to the European Social Policy'.

In cooperation with the European Trade Union Institute, he published *A Decade of Experience with the European Company* (ETUI, with Sigurt Vitols and Michael Stollt, 2013) and contributed to the ETUI's 'Sustainable Company' trilogy (2011–2015). Currently, he is the co-author of a book series focussing on workers' participation rights laid down in EU company law. The first volume is on workers' involvement under the EU Takeover Bids Directive (ETUI, October 2016), and the second volume is on workers' rights in merger processes (ETUI, April 2019).

The author wishes to thank Steven Jellinghaus for his contribution.

The Author

Table of Contents

The Author 3

List of Abbreviations 9

Part I. Implementation into National Law 11

Chapter 1. Legal Sources 11

Chapter 2. Objective and Scope 13

§1. Objective 13

§2. Scope 14
I. Territorial Scope 14
II. Personal Scope 15
III. Community-Scale Undertaking 15
IV. Community-Scale Groups of Undertakings 16

§3. General Principles 17
I. Information and Consultation 17
II. Representation of Employees 18

Chapter 3. Negotiation of the Agreement 21

§1. Parties to the Agreement 21
I. The SNB 21
II. The Central Management 22

§2. Negotiations 23
I. The Opening of Negotiations 23
II. Negotiation Procedure 23
III. Information of Local Employee Representatives 24

§3. Refusal and Termination without Result 25

§4. Experts 26

§5. Role of Trade Unions and Employers' Organisations 26

§6. Right of Appeal during the Negotiations 27

Chapter 4. The EWC 28

§1. The EWC Established by Agreement 28
I. Nature, Form and Scope of the Agreement 28
II. Rules of Procedure, Confidentiality and Content of the Agreement 28
III. Termination, Expiring and Renegotiation 30

§2. The EWC According to the Subsidiary Requirements 31
I. Applicability and Enforcement of the Subsidiary Requirements 31
II. Composition of the EWC 32
III. Internal Organisation, Select Committee 32
IV. Facilities, Resources, Costs 33
V. Meetings with the Central Management 33
VI. Competences of the EWC 34
VII. Significant Structural Changes 35
VIII. Experts, Trade Unions and Employers' Associations 35
IX. Confidentiality 35
X. Renegotiation 36

§3. Status of Employees' Representativeness 36
I. Working Time, Wage, Training and Facilities 36
II. Legal Protection 37
III. Relationship Between EWC and Local Employees' Representatives 39

Chapter 5. Pre-existing Agreements 40

Chapter 6. Coverage, Compliance and Enforcement 42

Chapter 7. Implementation of Directive 2009/38/EC (the 'Recast') 45

Part II. The Act on European Works Councils and the Recast Situated in the National Juridical Frame 47

Chapter 1. The Dutch Works Council Act (WOR) 47

Chapter 2. Other Relevant Parts of the Acquis 50

Chapter 3. Impact and Complementary Effect 52

Part III. The EWC Directive as Transposed into National Law 55
a. EWC Act of 23 January 1997 56
b. EWC Act: Amendments of 7 November 2011 70
c. EWC Act of 7 November 2011: Consolidated Version 79

Part IV. Selected Agreements 97
a. Introductory remarks, facts and figures 98
b. Océ – installation agreement 1996 100
c. Unilever – installation agreement 1996 104
d. Akzo Nobel – installation agreement 1997 110
e. TNT – renegotiated agreement 2011 119
f. Akzo Nobel – renegotiated agreement 2012 132
g. Unilever – renegotiated agreement 2014 144

Selected Bibliography 155

Index 157

List of Abbreviations

EWC	European Works Council
EWC Directive	Council Directive 94/45/EC of 22 September 1994 on the establishment of a European Works Council or a procedure in Community-scale undertakings and Community-scale groups of undertakings for the purposes of informing and consulting employees
EWC Recast Directive	Directive 2009/38/EC of the European Parliament and of the Council, 6 May 2009 on the establishment of a European Works Council or a procedure in Community-scale undertakings and Community-scale groups of undertakings for the purposes of informing and consulting employees
MVT 2011	Memorie van Toelichting (Explanatory Memorandum) – of the Act of 7 November 2011 amending the European Works Councils Act regarding the implementation of Directive 2009/38/EC of the European Parliament and of the Council of 6 May 2009 (OJ 122/2009) recasting Council Directive 94/45/EC
SE/SCE Act	Wet rol werknemers bij Europese rechtspersonen (Dutch Act on the workers' representation in European Company Statutes) – the integrated Act of 17 March 2005, implementing Council Directive 2001/86/EC of 8 October 2001 supplementing the Statute for a European company with regard to the involvement of employees (the SE Directive) and Council Directive 2003/72/EC of 22 July 2003 supplementing the Statute for a European Cooperative Society with regard to the involvement of employees (the SCE Directive)

List of Abbreviations

SNB	Special negotiating body, a group of employee representatives set up for the purpose of entering into negotiations with the management of an undertaking concerning an agreement on establishing a European Works Council or on making other arrangements for providing information to and consulting employees or their representatives on transnational matters
WEOR	Wet op de Europese Ondernemingsraden (Dutch European Works Council Act) – Act of 7 November 2011 amending the European Works Councils Act regarding the implementation of Directive 2009/38/EC of the European Parliament and of the Council of 6 May 2009 (OJ 122/2009) recasting Council Directive 94/45/EC (consolidated version – *see* Chapter 14).
WEOR 1997	Wet op de Europese Ondernemingsraden (Dutch European Works Council Act) – Act of 23 January 1997 for the implementation of Council Directive 94/45/EC of 22 September 1994 on the establishment of a European Works Council or a procedure in Community-scale undertakings and Community-scale groups of undertakings for the purposes of informing and consulting employees.
WOR	Wet op de ondernemingsraden (Dutch Works Council Act) – Act of 28 January 1971, containing provisions for the co-decision of workers in an undertaking through works councils.[1]

1. The Social Economic Council SER published an English version of the WOR: https://www.ser.nl/~/media/files/internet/talen/engels/2013/works-councils-act.ashx.

Part I. Implementation into National Law

Chapter 1. Legal Sources

1. The 1994 European Works Council Directive (Council Directive 94/45/EC of 22 September 1994 on the establishment of a European Works Council (EWC) or a procedure in Community-scale undertakings and Community-scale groups of undertakings for the purposes of informing and consulting employees, hereinafter 'the EWC Directive') was implemented in the Netherlands by the Act of 23 January 1997 concerning the establishment of an EWC or a procedure in Community-scale undertakings and Community-scale groups of undertakings for the purposes of informing and consulting employees (*Wet op de Europese Ondernemingsraden*, European Works Councils Act, hereinafter 'WEOR 1997').[2]

2. The Dutch legislator finalised the implementation shortly after the deadline of 22 September 1996, prescribed in Article 14(1) of Directive 94/45/EC. A first draft of the Act was formulated and handed over to the Dutch Parliament on 14 March 1996.[3] The parliamentarians formulated a series of amendments, related to, for instance, the use of experts, the frequency of meetings, the legal protection of EWC members, the defined competences and confidentiality issues.

3. Over the years, the Dutch legislator introduced minor corrections and changes. In 1998, the numbering of Articles 3–5 was corrected; on 25 April 1999, the integration of the UK was formulated in the WEOR 1997; in 2001, the wording of Article 5 was corrected; in 2010, the wording of Article 2 was corrected.[4]

4. An important change was decided in 2005, during the implementation of the Council Directive 2001/86/EC of 8 October 2001 supplementing the Statute for a European company with regard to the involvement of employees and Council Directive 2003/72/EC of 22 July 2003 supplementing the Statute for a European Cooperative Society with regard to the involvement of employees. In the slipstream of this implementation, a modification of the WEOR 1997 created the possibility for

2. At http://wetten.overheid.nl/BWBR0008508/2013-01-01.
3. At https://zoek.officielebekendmakingen.nl/behandelddossier/24641/kst-24641-1?resultIndex=38&sorttype=1&sortorder=4.
4. At http://wetten.overheid.nl/BWBR0008508/2013-01-01/0/afdrukken+informatie.

EWCs to appeal to the Enterprise Chamber of the Amsterdam Court in well-defined cases, such as the proportionality of confidentiality measures and the lack of information.

5. The WEOR 1997 was revised after the adoption of the EWC Recast Directive (Directive 2009/38/EC of the European Parliament and of the Council, 6 May 2009 on the establishment of an EWC or a procedure in Community-scale undertakings and Community-scale groups of undertakings for the purposes of informing and consulting employees, hereinafter 'EWC Recast Directive').

6. In the memorandum, which explained the implementation of the EWC Recast Directive[5], the Dutch legislator stated that, for reasons of consistency, it was its aim to use as much as possible the terminology, which was applied for the existing Act (WEOR 1997), the Dutch Works Council Act (WOR) and the Act on the workers' representation in European Company Statutes (SE/SCE Act).[6]

7. The amendments led to a 'revised' WEOR that was presented to the Second Chamber on 28 March 2011 and finalised on 7 November 2011. The legislation came into effect on 15 November 2011, after the publication in the Official Journal.[7] With the acceptance of this Act, the WEOR 1997 was repealed. After the publication of the WEOR in 2011, a minor modification was introduced in December 2011.

8. The implementation in 2017 of Directive (EU) 2015/1794 of the European Parliament and of the Council of 6 October 2015 amending Directives 2008/94/EC, 2009/38/EC and 2002/14/EC of the European Parliament and of the Council, and Council Directives 98/59/EC and 2001/23/EC, as regards seafarers, led to the introduction of the attendance of seafarers in EWC activities. As a consequence, Article 10.7 of the WEOR was deleted (on 29 November 2017).

9. Chapter 10 provides an updated, consolidated version of the WEOR with the amendments from 1997 to 2021. The UK withdrawal has not led to amendments of the WEOR.

---

5. The MVT 2011 (in Dutch – *Memorie van Toelichting*): https://www.rijksoverheid.nl/documenten/kamerstukken/2011/03/22/memorie-van-toelichting-wijziging-wet-europese-ondernemingsraden.
6. Wet rol werknemers bij Europese rechtspersonen: http://wetten.overheid.nl/BWBR0018115/2013-01-01.
7. Wijziging Wet op de Europese ondernemingsraden. Uitvoering van richtlijn 2009/38/EG van het Europees Parlement en de Raad van de Europese Unie van 6 mei 2009 (PbEU 2009, L 122), houdende herschikking van richtlijn 94/45/EG, inzake de instelling van een Europese ondernemingsraad of van een procedure in ondernemingen of concerns met een communautaire dimensie ter informatie en raadpleging van de werknemers (*Staatsblad*, 14 November 2011).

Chapter 2. Objective and Scope

§1. OBJECTIVE

10. The Dutch legislator decided to implement the EWC Directives in standalone legislation. The legislator synchronised in 1997 the scope of the existing Dutch legislation on information, consultation and co-decision with the scope of the EWC Directive by incorporating the provisions into a separate act, i.e., the European Works Councils Act (WEOR 1997). The transposition in 2011 of the EWC Recast Directive led to modifications of the earlier act, combined with unchanged provisions. An alternative possibility had been to incorporate the EWC Directives into the Dutch legal system by means of a new chapter in the existing national act on works councils (hereinafter WOR). This alternative was not chosen.

11. Nevertheless, we find that the WOR and the WEOR regularly run parallel and this was also the government's objective. Directive 94/45/EC prescribed in Article 12 that the '... Directive shall be without prejudice to employees' existing rights to information and consultation under national law'. *Inter alia*, this is reflected in the system chosen and the terms used. In the 2011 explanatory memorandum (hereinafter 'MVT 2011'), it is said that the government considers the EWC Directives to be complementary and supportive to the co-decision of workers as enshrined in the WOR.[8] The legislator refers herewith implicitly to Article 12.1 of the EWC Recast Directive ('Information and consultation of the EWC shall be linked to those of the national employee representation bodies, with due regard to the competences and areas of action').

12. Article 14.1 of the Council Directive 94/45/EC of 22 September 1994 on the establishment of an EWC or a procedure in Community-scale undertakings and Community-scale groups of undertakings for the purposes of informing and consulting employees prescribes that 'Member States shall bring into force the laws, regulations and administrative provisions necessary to comply with this Directive no later than 22 September 1996 or shall ensure by that date at the latest that management and labour introduce the required provisions by way of agreement, the Member States being obliged to take all necessary steps enabling them at all times to guarantee the results imposed by this Directive.' The objective of the WEOR 1997 was to ensure a proper transposition and implementation of the EWC Directive (94/45/EC).

13. Article 16(1) of Directive 2009/38/EC of the European Parliament and of the Council of 6 May 2009 (OJ 122/2009) recasting Council Directive 94/45/EC prescribes that the Member States shall bring into force the laws, regulations and administrative provisions necessary to comply with different articles of the Directive 2009/38/EC, no later than 5 June 2011. In view of this transposition, the WEOR

8. The MVT 2011, page 10. The legislator implements herewith Art. 12.1 of the EWC Recast Directive ('Information and consultation of the European Works Council shall be linked to those of the national employee representation bodies, with due regard to the competences and areas of action').

1997 was changed into the Act of 7 November 2011, with the aim to properly amend a number of provisions. The implementation of the EWC Recast Directive was mainly a technical exercise; it had little or no consequences for the substance of the legislation.[9]

14. The legislator combined some material changes with the other unchanged provisions in a new text and repealed the old act. The guiding principles and main objectives for the implementation were taken from Article 1.2 of the EWC Recast Directive:

> The arrangements for informing and consulting employees shall be defined and implemented in such a way as to ensure their effectiveness and to enable the undertaking or group of undertakings to take decisions effectively.[10]

§2. Scope

I. Territorial Scope

15. The Dutch legislator has revised the wording of the overall scope during the implementation of the EWC Recast Directive. In the WEOR 1997, the wording 'Member States' was used to indicate the territorial scope, meaning a Member State of the European Union or another State, which is party to the Agreement on the European Economic Area. In the wording of the currently applicable WEOR, 'Member States' has been replaced by the notion 'Involved State'. In practice, this still means that the Dutch legislation applies to the EU Member States as well as to the countries that are part of the European Economic Area.[11]

16. The provisions of the Dutch WEOR 2011 apply to Community-scale undertakings or controlling undertakings, which maintain their registered office or their

9. Verburg, L.G. (2009) 'De herschikking van de EOR-Richtlijn', TRA 2009/43. Gerlach V. and Broeckhuijsen M.P. van, (2012) De gewijzigde Wet op de Europese Ondernemingsraden: business as usual, ArbeidsRecht 2012/5.
10. As quoted in the MVT 2011: https://www.rijksoverheid.nl/documenten/kamerstukken/2011/03/22/memorie-van-toelichting-wijziging-wet-europese-ondernemingsraden.
11. These are the twenty-seven EU Member States: Austria; Belgium; Bulgaria; Croatia; Cyprus; the Czech Republic; Denmark; Estonia; Finland; France; Germany; Greece; Hungary; Ireland; Italy; Latvia; Lithuania; Luxembourg; Malta; the Netherlands; Poland; Portugal; Rumania; Slovenia; Slovakia; Spain; Sweden; and the EEA Member States: Liechtenstein, Norway and Iceland (situation in 2017). As of the withdrawal date (30 March 2019), the United Kingdom is considered to be a 'third country'. The EU rules in the field of information and consultation of workers at transnational level, i.e., Directive 2009/38/EC on European Works Councils, no longer apply. The UK is no longer counted as a Member State and employees in the UK no longer count as employees within the Member States.

central seat in the Netherlands. Where the domicile of a Community-scale undertaking or controlling undertaking is not situated in any involved State, several sections of the WEOR shall apply if the domicile or headquarters of the establishment or group undertaking as referred to in Article 1(2) and (3) is situated in the Netherlands.

17. The European Works Councils Act also applies to Community-scale groups of undertakings in which the parent or group undertaking has its residence or registered office in the Netherlands.

II. Personal Scope

18. With regard to the personal scope, the person who is working in the Netherlands for the Community-scale undertaking or group on the basis of an employment agreement qualifies as an employee. Based on the WOR, part-time workers are considered and calculated in the WEOR as full-time employees. The work relationship does not necessarily need to be an employment agreement under the Dutch law. For employees not working within the Netherlands, there is a reference to persons defined as such under the law of the relevant Involved State.[12]

III. Community-Scale Undertaking

19. The WEOR obligates any so-called Community-scale undertaking to establish an EWC. Thus, this concerns an initiative taken by the Community-scale undertaking. Moreover, there is the obligation in Article 15 of the WEOR to establish such an EWC if this has not been done voluntarily within six months after a request has been made to this effect. In such a situation, the undertaking should initiate a special negotiating body (hereinafter SNB) within three years after deciding not to establish an EWC by itself.

20. The obligation to establish an EWC is incumbent on a so-called Community-scale undertaking that meets several conditions for the duration of at least two years.[13] The undertaking must exercise control over at least two undertakings that are situated in different Involved States. During this period, one undertaking must have had an average of at least 150 employees in one Involved State and another undertaking must have had an average of at least 150 employees in another Involved State. All the undertakings taken together should have had for these two years an average of at least 1,000 employees in the Involved States. If it meets these accumulative requirements, it qualifies as a so-called Community-scale undertaking, which is obligated to establish an EWC.

12. Article 3.1 WEOR.
13. Article 1.1 sub c WEOR.

21. It is possible that an undertaking from outside the Community complies with the criteria to establish an EWC inside the Community. In that case, the largest group undertaking in terms of the number of employees within a Member State has the obligation of establishment.[14] There can always and only be just one undertaking accountable.[15]

IV. Community-Scale Groups of Undertakings

22. This gives rise to the question of how a conglomerate, i.e., a group of undertakings, should be addressed. The EWC Directives speak about a Community-scale group of undertakings. This Community-scale group is defined as a cluster of undertakings that is (in summary) under the control of a parent company.[16] The question of whether an undertaking belongs to a group depends on the exercise of decisive control. This condition implies a legal presumption, which means that it is up to the undertaking to prove the opposite (a reversal of the burden of proof). The Dutch legislator did not use the term 'controlling undertaking' for the Dutch language version of the Directive but used the word 'parent undertaking'. Legal history shows that these terms have the same meaning.[17]

23. An undertaking is presumed to be a controlling company, if it:

(a) can appoint more than half of the members of the other undertaking's administrative, management or supervisory body; or
(b) can exercise over half of the voting rights at the general meeting of that other undertaking; or
(c) holds over 50% of another undertaking's subscribed capital.[18]

24. A controlling undertaking's rights as regards capital, voting and appointment shall include:

(a) the corresponding rights of other undertakings over which it exercises a dominant influence;
(b) the corresponding rights of any person or body acting in his or its own name but for account of the controlling undertaking or of one or more of its group undertakings.[19]

14. *See* Parliamentary Papers 24.641, no. 11 for an amendment; also HvJ 13 January 2004, C440/00.
15. Enterprise Chamber of the Amsterdam Court of Appeal, 1 April 2004, ARO 2004/51.
16. Article 1.1 sub d WEOR.
17. Parliamentary Papers II 24.641, no. 3, p. 18.
18. Article 2.1 WEOR.
19. Article 2.2 WEOR.

25. Scholars see this as a purely legal approach to the controlling relationship, which does not pay attention to management considerations.[20] However, the 'central management' of an undertaking is responsible for the implementation of the regulation. This refers to the management of parent undertakings and of groups of undertakings.[21]

26. When an undertaking holds capital rights and the voting power for others, this is not attributed to the undertaking. Pledged voting power is attributed to the pledge holder. Nor does an undertaking as referred to in Article 3(5) at (a) or (c) of Council Regulation (EEC) No. 139/2004 of 20 January 2004 on the control of concentrations between undertakings (OJ L 24/2004) qualifies as a parent undertaking.[22]

27. Where various undertakings within a group meet the criteria to qualify as a parent undertaking, the undertaking that can appoint more than half the members of the administrative body, or of the management or supervisory body of the other undertaking, qualifies as the parent undertaking. If this does not result in one undertaking qualifying as the parent undertaking, the following order applies:

- the undertaking that can exercise over half of the voting rights at the general meeting of the other undertaking;
- the undertaking that holds over 50% of another undertaking's subscribed capital.[23]

§3. General Principles

I. Information and Consultation

28. The WEOR 2011, based on the EWC Recast Directive, defines (the provision of) information as:

> 'Provision of information' means the transmission of information concerning cross-border issues by the central management or any more appropriate level of management to employees' representatives at such time, in such fashion and with such content as are appropriate to enable employees' representatives to undertake an in-depth assessment of the impact and, where appropriate, to prepare for consultations with the central management or any more appropriate level of management.

20. Bijll Nachenius, H.J. de, (1996), Wet op de Europese Ondernemingsraden, De NV, 1996, 74/5, pp. 132–133.
21. Parliamentary Papers II 24.641, no. 3, p. 19.
22. Article 2.5 WEOR.
23. This involves a legal presumption. An undertaking may possibly demonstrate that another undertaking has decisive influence and that for that reason that undertaking qualifies as a parent undertaking.

29. This definition includes notions that specify certain elements of the definition as formulated in Article 2 of the EWC Recast Directive. First of all, the EU Directive uses the word 'information', whilst the Dutch legislator comes with the more specific 'provision of information'. Second, the information has to be provided by 'the central management or any more appropriate level of management', instead of the 'employer' (as formulated in the EU Directives). Third, the Dutch legislator talks about information that enables employees' representatives to prepare for 'consultations with the central management or any more appropriate level of management', instead of 'consultations with the competent organ of the Community-scale undertaking or Community-scale group of undertakings'. This confirms and clarifies the key responsibility of the central management.

30. With reference to the EWC Recast Directive, the WEOR 2011 defines consultation as:

> 'Consultation' means the establishment of dialogue and exchange of views between the central management or any more appropriate level of management and employees' representatives at such time, in such fashion and with such content enabling employees' representatives to express an opinion on the basis of the information provided about proposed measures concerning cross-border issues to which the consultation relates within a reasonable time, which may be taken into account when a decision is taken.

31. This definition adds to the EU EWC Directive's definition of consultation the notion that an advice 'may be taken into account when a decision is taken'. One could conclude, therefore, that the Dutch legislator refers explicitly to EWC opinions as contributions to the decision-making in an undertaking.

II. Representation of Employees

32. The notion of 'employee representative' appears in several articles of the WEOR and is relevant in various situations. It is noteworthy that Article 1 of the WEOR, which deals with definitions, does not provide an overall definition of the term 'employee representative'. The legislator has chosen for a different approach as the notion is formulated for several specific features.

33. The first feature is the situation related to the membership of an SNB. Article 10 prescribes that with regard to Dutch establishments and undertakings, the members of the SNB shall be appointed, or their appointment terminated, by the joint works councils set up at these establishments or undertakings (or their central works councils if these bodies exist).[24] If no Dutch Works Council exists, the members of

24. According to the national Works Council Act (WOR), every Dutch undertaking, employing fifty or more workers, has to establish a representative workers instance which deals with information, consultation and co-decision rights that are enshrined in the WOR. *See*: Drongelen, J. van and S.F.H.

the SNB shall be elected by secret written ballot by the entire body of employees working in the Netherlands for the Community-scale undertaking or group; in this case every worker has one vote.[25] It is generally assumed that a confidential digital ballot is allowable. Trade unions that have stipulated in their statutes that they represent the employees' interests are entitled to submit a list of candidates under the condition that they have members within the undertaking. Thus, the national representative bodies (or, in the absence, the workforce) are free to elect or nominate the representative(s) in the SNB. As a consequence, the membership of an SNB is open for representatives that are not working for the undertaking, such as trade union officers.[26]

34. Article 3.2 provides another specific feature as this article clarifies the reference to 'employee representatives' in several articles of the WEOR that deal with the justification of certain activities. According to Article 3.2 'employees' representatives' means for the purpose of certain parts of the WEOR those persons defined as such under the law of the Involved State in which the employees are working; in the case of the Netherlands it means works councils.[27] The consequences of this specific definition are that the initiative to open negotiations and the right to receive the necessary information for the opening is reserved for employees or employee representatives working for the undertakings and reporting on progress shall always take place to national works council members, or in the absence of works councils, all employees, on the other hand. The WEOR specifies the concept of employee representative also in the context of the final composition of the European representative instance; the membership is restricted to employees of the Community-scale undertaking or group.[28]

35. If an undertaking has both units with and without works councils, the employees who are not represented by a works council are given the opportunity to give their views about the persons who are to be appointed as members of the special negotiating body. This may include business units that do not have fifty or more

---

Jellinghaus, Wet op de ondernemingsraden, Paris 2014, Vink, F. and R. van het Kaar, Inzicht in de ondernemingsraad, SDU 2017 and Verburg, L., Rood's Wet op de ondernemingsraden, Kluwer 2013.

25. Article 10 WEOR provides an order of priority: members of the SNB are appointed by the central works councils (10.2), if there are no overarching central works councils, by one or more group works councils (10.3) or if not all (group) works councils are covered by central works councils, jointly by central works councils, group works councils and the non-represented works councils (10.4). If no works council has been set up, the members of the special negotiating body shall be elected by the entire body of employees working in the Netherlands for the Community-scale undertaking or group (10.5). Employees of Dutch establishments or undertakings who are not represented in a works council, group works council or central works council will be given the opportunity to express an opinion about the persons to be appointed (10.6).
26. Stoop S. et al., 2011, De Europese ondernemingsraad – Een handboek voor de praktijk, Alphen aan de Rijn.
27. Reference is made to the notion of employee representatives for the purpose of Art. 4 eighth to tenth subsections, Art. 7, Art. 8 second subsection and Art. 11, third subsection (e), sixth subsection and eighth subsection of the WEOR.
28. This notion is spread over several articles, Art. 3, Art. 4, Art. 7 and Art. 17.2 WEOR. As a consequence, EWC membership ends when a member ceases to be an employee.

employees. In such a case, a so-called personal representation (Dutch abbreviation – pvt) might exist, which may then have the possibility to give a view about the delegation elected from the works councils.

36. The position of employee representatives who are merchant seafarers has been subject to special legislation. Originally, the WEOR 1997 excluded employee representatives who were merchant seafarers from the application of the WEOR, both with regard to the membership of the SNB and of the negotiated EWC, with the argument that they operated very often too far away from the management and central premises.[29] This changed after the implementation in 2017 of Directive (EU) 2015/1794 of the European Parliament and of the Council of 6 October 2015 amending Directives 2008/94/EC, 2009/38/EC and 2002/14/EC of the European Parliament and of the Council, and Council Directives 98/59/EC and 2001/23/EC, as regards seafarers, led to the introduction of the attendance of seafarers in EWC activities. The sentence in the WEOR 1997 that stated, in Article 17.2, 'Persons who are seafarers in the merchant navy shall not be appointed or elected as members' has been deleted. Article 17.2 that excluded these employees from the negotiations or the functioning of an EWC was modified. In the WEOR 2011, the possibility for seafarers is opened up, in a new Article 17.3, to attend under certain circumstances meetings of both the SNB and the EWC.[30]

37. For the employee representatives from the different involved countries, the WEOR prescribes that for representatives to become a member of the SNB, they 'shall be elected or appointed pursuant to the law of the Involved State in which he works'. The same condition is formulated for the membership of the EWC: 'each member shall be elected or appointed pursuant to the law of the Involved State in which he works'.[31]

38. If, in an involved State other than the Netherlands, a special negotiating body is set up in a Community-scale undertaking or group, the provisions of Articles 10 and 17 that regulate the SNB membership (appointment, election or termination) apply mutatis mutandis to Dutch establishments or undertakings in that Community-scale undertaking or group.[32]

---

29. Parliamentary Papers 24.641, no. 8.
30. Article 17.3 WEOR says: A member of the special negotiating body or of the European Works Councils and his/her deputy, who is seafarer in the merchant navy, have the right to attend the meetings of the special negotiating body or the European Works Council or any other consultation that is organised, if the member or deputy is not offshore or in a harbour in another State than the State of establishment of the shipping company. As far as possible, the meeting will be planned in such a manner that the member or the deputy can easily attend. In case the member or deputy cannot attend the meeting, an effort will be made to receive input of the member or deputy by other means.
31. Respectively in Arts 9.2 and 16.2 of the WEOR.
32. Article 23 WEOR.

Chapter 3. Negotiation of the Agreement

§1. Parties to the Agreement

39. There are two possible ways to establish an EWC. First, an EWC can be established through a (negotiated) agreement, or second (if there is no agreement) the subsidiary requirements governing the provision of information and consultation in the absence of an agreement apply.[33] This chapter deals with the negotiations, the establishment through the subsidiary requirements is treated later on in Chapter 4, §2 *The EWC According to the Subsidiary Requirements* (paragraph 76–94).

40. In accordance with Article 7 WEOR, the Community-scale undertaking is obligated to supply the employees or their representatives with the information needed to start negotiations in order to establish an EWC. The information to be presented is limited to information that is absolutely indispensable for the start of the negotiations.[34] This information should at least include the number of employees working at the undertaking or group, and the distribution of those employees among the various Involved States.[35] This obligation also refers to the subsidiaries.[36]

41. Article 8 WEOR provides the criteria that are decisive for the set-up of negotiations in the frame of an EWC procedure. The starting point is whether an undertaking meets the prescribed criteria for establishing an EWC. Every employee working in the Netherlands, or his/her representative (such as a union), may require that he or she shall be given the information needed to verify whether the necessary criteria to open negotiations are met. These provisions have been included in the act, in order to make it possible for employees, or unions, to conclude that the undertaking falls under the scope of the WEOR.

I. The SNB

42. If an undertaking has to apply the WEOR and establish an EWC, negotiations are at stake. These talks will take place within the so-called special negotiating body. The central management of a Community-scale undertaking or group established in the Netherlands shall start these negotiations at the request of at least 100 employees or their representatives. These employees must work in at least two countries that are part of the scope of the EWC Directives.

33. The subsidiary requirements are not formulated in an Annex but are part of the WEOR text (Arts 15–22).
34. European Court of Justice 15 June 2004, C-349/01, JOR 2004/267 and European Court of Justice, 29 March 2001, C62/99, JOR 2001/143.
35. Article 4.9 WEOR.
36. Parliamentary Papers 24.641, no. 8.

43. During the implementation of the EWC Recast Directive, a new provision was introduced related to substantial changes in the corporate structure. Negotiations may be opened to achieve an agreement (or a replacement of an existing agreement) if the corporate structure of the Community-scale undertaking or group changes drastically. The central administration shall, on its own initiative or at the written request of at least 100 employees or their representatives in at least two companies or establishments in at least two different relevant States, start the negotiations and shall set up an SNB for this purpose.[37]

44. The special negotiating body consists of representatives of employees working at the Community-scale undertaking or group. For the Netherlands, a member of a works council qualifies as the employee representative, for other countries, election or appointment is subject to the law of the involved State in which he or she works.[38]

45. Per Member State, one member must be elected or appointed for every 10% (or a fraction thereof) of the employees working in the Member State concerned. This is calculated in proportion to the total number of employees working at the undertaking or group. If the number of employees in a Member State should change, the voting rights of the delegation shall be adjusted accordingly.[39] Every member has a vote unless the ratio alters due to changes in staff numbers.[40]

46. The procedure for the election or nomination of Dutch members of SNBs in non-Dutch Community-scale undertakings or groups has to take place according to the same provisions in the WEOR. The employer of an employee who is working in the Netherlands and is appointed or elected as an SNB member shall report such appointment or election to the central management.[41] In return, the central management has to ensure that the composition of the special negotiating body is made known within the Community-scale undertaking or group.[42]

II. The Central Management

47. The central management has the duty to give information about the composition of the special negotiating body within the Community-scale undertaking or

37. Article 14a of the WEOR. In case an existing agreement is renegotiated, the composition of the SNB is partially prescribed (at least three members of the existing European Works Council shall be SNB members).
38. Article 9.1 and 9.2.
39. Article 9.3 WEOR.
40. Article 13 WEOR.
41. Article 4.10 WEOR.
42. Article 14.1 WEOR.

group (including the trade unions) as well as the date and time of the first meeting. This refers to both the trade unions and the employers' organisations that are registered at the Community level.[43]

§2. NEGOTIATIONS

I. The Opening of Negotiations

48. As soon as a special negotiating body has been established, the central management will hold a meeting aimed at negotiating an agreement. The central management provides the negotiating body with the opportunity to meet before and after this meeting. The legislator gives the parties a great deal of scope to negotiate an agreement. Parties are free to determine the negotiation process, the subjects that they want to deal with, the frequency and forms of negotiations and the possible results, with the exception of a number of subjects that are prescribed for an agreement (this will be treated in Chapter 4). The only restriction is the total duration; if no agreement is reached within a three-year period after the establishment of an SNB, the central management shall be obliged to apply the subsidiary requirements.[44]

II. Negotiation Procedure

49. The objective of the negotiations is to come to an agreement on the provision of information and consultation for employees and their representatives about any cross-border issue. The special negotiating body has the task of determining, with the central management, by written agreement, the scope, composition, functions and term of office of the EWC(s) or the arrangements for implementing a procedure for the information and consultation of employees. The WEOR does not contain general clauses for the conduct of the parties. Thus, it is up to the central management and the SNB to agree upon the dates, the frequency and the location where the negotiations shall take place. Neither in the WEOR nor in the MVT 2011 of the national transposition there is a reference to specific procedures that could contribute to the ambitions mentioned in Recital 7 of the EWC Recast Directive.[45]

50. However, the WEOR prescribes a series of facilities that serve to come to an agreement. During the negotiations, the SNB members retain their entitlement to payment for the period of absence from work necessary to attend a meeting of the

43. Article 14.2 of the WEOR refers to 'the authorised and recognised employee and employers' organisations at Community level, as provided for in Article 154 of the Treaty on the Functioning of the European Union'.
44. Article 15 WEOR.
45. The European legislator motivated the EWC Recast Directive with the argument that a new dynamic for negotiations had to be created. Recital 7 speaks about the ambition to increase 'the proportion of European Works Councils established'.

special negotiating body (Article 4.2). They shall be afforded the possibility – during working hours and without loss of pay – of taking part in mutual consultations and deliberations with other persons on matters concerning the performance of their duties, and of undergoing education and training (Article 4.3). They may make use of the undertakings' facilities, within reasonable limits.[46] Any costs that are incurred to exercise the function of SNB member shall be borne by the Community-scale undertaking or the controlling undertaking (Article 12.2). Overall, SNB members shall be provided with such facilities, which they reasonably need for the performance of their duties. Moreover, they shall not suffer any disadvantage in their position within the undertaking for their activity as SNB member (Article 4.7).

51. The WEOR formulates in Article 13 rules and procedures for the decision-making in the SNB. Each SNB member shall have one vote. Decisions shall be adopted by an absolute majority of the number of votes cast, except for the decision not to enter into negotiations or to terminate negotiations already in progress. The decision to refrain from negotiations must be adopted by a two-thirds majority of the number of votes cast. The decision to conclude an agreement requires at least a majority of all the votes of the total number that can be cast at a plenary meeting of the SNB.[47]

III. Information of Local Employee Representatives

52. The information of local employee representatives is guaranteed in several ways. First of all, there are obligations, before and during the negotiations, for the central management related to the necessary information, the composition of the SNB and the negotiation process. Second, one could argue that the WEOR obliges the directly involved employee representatives to inform the local representatives about the outcome of the negotiations (after the installation of an EWC).

53. The central management provides employees or their representatives with:

- the information, necessary for employee representatives to open negotiations;
- significant changes of information after the establishment of the special negotiating body, as quickly as possible after such change, in a revised overview to the special negotiating body and, where appropriate, to the employees or the representatives of employees.

Moreover, the central management ensures that the composition of the SNB and the time of any meeting are made known within the Community-scale undertaking or group.

---

46. The MVT 2011 speaks about the facility to meet, the provision of communication methods and facilities, the translation of documents.
47. Article 11.1 and 11.2 and Art. 13.1–13.2 WEOR.

54. There is no hard legal obligation in the WEOR for SNB members to report the outcome of the negotiations to local employees and their representatives.[48] Apparently, the Dutch legislator assumes it is self-evident that the explicit link with the Dutch system of work councils guarantees the necessary reporting.[49] However, in general terms, members of an EWC or representatives under any other procedure for informing and consulting employees shall inform the employee representatives within the Community-scale undertaking or group of undertakings or, if these do not exist, all the employees about the content of the information and consultation procedure.[50]

55. SNB members are bound by confidentiality on all business and company secrets which come to their knowledge in their capacity as a member of the special negotiating body as well as on all matters designated confidential or whose confidential nature they ought to appreciate in the light of the confidentiality requirement imposed. The duty of confidentiality does not cease after the termination of the membership of the SNB.[51]

§3. Refusal and Termination without Result

56. The special negotiating body can take the decision not to enter into negotiations or to terminate negotiations already in progress, as long as no agreement has been concluded.[52] Another reason for the absence of or failure to attain a negotiated agreement is the refusal of the central management to enter into negotiations, within six months after a request from the employee side to set up an SNB was formulated. The third reason can be that the central management and the SNB do not reach an agreement within a stipulated period of three years after the receipt of a request to set up an SNB, or, within three years, if the central management has established an SNB of its own accord.[53, 54]

---

48. In line with Recital 33 of the EWC Recast Directive ('In order to perform their representative role fully and to ensure that the European Works Council is useful, employees' representatives must report to the employees whom they represent'), one would have expected an obligation for SNB members to report about the outcome of the negotiations.
49. The MVT 2011 refers to Article 3.2 of the WEOR, where it is said that 'employees' representatives' in the case of the Netherlands means works councils. Other references are made to Art. 11.4 WEOR. However, this article only obliges to include in any alternative information and consultation procedure an arrangement how the employees or their representatives are to be informed and consulted on transnational questions which significantly affect employees' interests.
50. Article 4.8 WEOR can be read as an indirect obligation for EWC members to report to local employee representatives about the agreement resulting from negotiations after the installation of an EWC. This article prescribes that members of a European Works Council or representatives under any other procedure for informing and consulting employees shall inform the employee representatives within the Community-scale undertaking or group of undertakings or, if these do not exist, all the employees about the content of the information and consultation procedure.
51. Article 4.4 and 4.6 WEOR.
52. Article 11.2 WEOR.
53. Article 15.1 WEOR.
54. The Dutch legislator states in the MVT 2011 that it is in practice rather rare that no agreement can be reached.

57. In all the three cases, the central management has to apply the subsidiary requirements of the WEOR.[55] These requirements are treated in Chapter 4.2 *The EWC According to the Subsidiary Requirements.*

§4. Experts

58. The SNB members may be assisted during the negotiations by one or more experts of their choice, including representatives of authorised and recognised employee organisations at the Community level, as provided for in Article 154 of the Treaty on the Functioning of the European Union. These experts may, at the request of the SNB, attend the negotiations. The expenses of consulting one or more experts have to be borne only if the Community-scale undertaking or the controlling undertaking has been notified in advance of the involved expenses.[56]

59. Experts brought in for consultation during the negotiations do not fall under the duty of confidentiality, provided that the central management or the person who has imposed a confidentiality requirement has given due approval beforehand and the person involved has declared in writing that he undertakes to observe confidentiality, if necessary.[57]

§5. Role of Trade Unions and Employers' Organisations

60. The WEOR introduces one special provision for the relevant employers' organisations and trade unions at European level, in the form of a notification obligation in the procedure. The central management shall notify 'the authorised and recognised employee and employers' organisations at the Community level, as provided for in Article 154 of the Treaty on the Functioning of the European Union', about the composition of the special negotiating body, and about the start of the negotiations.[58]

61. The most important role given to external trade union representatives (representatives of authorised and recognised employee organisations at the Community level, as provided for in Article 154 of the Treaty on the Functioning of the European Union) is the role of expert or SNB assistant in the negotiations.[59] The WEOR leaves it open whether the union representatives are coming from national or European trade union bodies. Like all other experts, these assistants may, at the request of the special negotiating body, attend all SNB meetings in an advisory capacity.[60]

---

55. The WEOR prescribes the subsidiary requirements in a separate paragraph (Arts 15–22).
56. Article 12 WEOR.
57. Article 4.5 WEOR.
58. Article 14.2 WEOR.
59. In the MVT 2011, the legislator says that the role of trade unions is explicitly recognised, particularly in an advisory capacity during the preparations and negotiations of an EWC agreement.
60. Article 12.1 WEOR.

§6. Right of Appeal during the Negotiations

62. The WEOR provides the SNB and its members with the right to appeal to the Enterprise Chamber of the Amsterdam Court. They can ask the Chamber to remove a prescribed confidentiality, on the ground that the person who has prescribed the confidentiality should not have decided, in all fairness, in the weighing up of all involved interests, to prescribe confidentiality. Moreover, they can request, through the intervention of the Chamber, the provision of refused information on the ground that the person should not have decided, in all fairness, in the weighing up of all involved interests, to refuse the information.[61]

63. If any legal proceedings are started by the SNB, the undertaking or group must be notified of the likely costs beforehand. These costs must also be reasonable. This will usually be the case, unless the hourly rate is excessive and/or a disproportionate number of hours is spent on the discussion of the file. Jurisdiction shows that the (legal) costs that are incurred as part of terminating the agreement are also included.[62]

---

61. Article 5.2 WEOR that was added in 2005, following the implementation of the Council Directive 2001/86/EC of 8 October 2001 supplementing the Statute for a European company with regard to the involvement of employees and Council Directive 2003/72/EC of 22 July 2003 supplementing the Statute for a European Cooperative Society with regard to the involvement of employees.
62. Amsterdam Court of Appeal, 1 April 2004, JAR 2004/110.

Chapter 4. The EWC

§1. The EWC Established by Agreement

64. The autonomy of the representatives from management and labour to negotiated wages, working conditions and other aspects of the working life is, in general, a key characteristic of the Dutch system of industrial relations. It fits in this tradition that the legislator refrains from a too strong influence on the content of negotiations and bargaining of private parties. And like been said before, the Dutch legislator has presumed that in most cases where negotiations are started, an agreement can be reached.[63]

I. Nature, Form and Scope of the Agreement

65. There is a difference in nature between the regulation of the national and the European information and consultation rights. In the field of national information and consultation, the legislator has developed in the aftermath of WW II a detailed regulatory frame for the functioning of works councils (WOR), which entails extensive information and consultation rights to workers representatives. The model chosen for EWCs has more the character of a contract model, with general principles and global rights. Nevertheless, the legislator is also aware of the fact that, for instance, the provisions listed in the subsidiary requirements might function as guidelines for the arrangements in (re)negotiated agreements.

66. An agreement established by negotiations is relatively undefined; parties are relatively free to determine the content as long as the objective of the agreement is making arrangements for providing information to and consulting employees or their representatives on transnational matters. Moreover, the parties can decide to install separate EWCs for different parts of the Community-scale undertaking or group, or to apply separate procedures. They may also agree to set up one or more EWCs for one or more parts of the Community-scale undertaking or group and introduce one or more procedures for other parts.[64]

II. Rules of Procedure, Confidentiality and Content of the Agreement

67. An agreement has to be recorded in writing and incorporates arrangements between the EWC and the Community-scale undertaking or group. It has to regulate at least:

(a) the establishments or undertakings of the Community-scale undertaking or group for which the EWC is being set up;

---

63. *See* note 52. The Dutch legislator also refers to the Impact assessment of the European Commission that was published with the draft of the EWC Recast Directive, SEC (2008) 2166, page 38.
64. Article 11.5 WEOR.

(b) the size and composition of the EWC, with as balanced a representation of workers as possible, and the period of appointment of its members;
(c) the EWC's scope and competence;
(d) the arrangements for informing and consulting the EWC;
(e) how the information and consultation of the EWC and the information and consultation of national employee representatives are linked together, taking into account their responsibilities;
(f) the frequency, duration and venue of EWC meetings;
(g) the financial and material resources to be placed at the EWC's disposal;
(h) if a select committee is set up within the EWC: its composition, appointment procedure, terms of reference and rules of procedure.[65]

68. If alternative arrangements for providing information to and consulting employees or their representatives are chosen, then these arrangements have also to be settled in an agreement that stipulates at least:

(a) the establishments or undertakings of the Community-scale undertaking or group to which the procedure applies;
(b) the way in which the employees or their representatives are to be informed and consulted on transnational questions which significantly affect employees' interests;
(c) the manner in which employees or their representatives may meet to discuss the questions referred to in point b;
(d) the financial and material resources made available to implement the procedure.[66]

69. The central management may impose an obligation of confidentiality on the EWC members if there is a reasonable cause. When this applies, the members will be informed of this obligation as long before the discussion of the issue at hand as possible and of the reason for it. Also, the central management must divulge which information is confidential, for how long a period the obligation of confidentiality obtains and with respect to which persons it need not be observed. Also, the central management need not give any information that would seriously impede or harm the functioning of the Community-scale undertaking or group. This also applies if no provisions to this effect have been included in the agreement. Obviously, normal confidentiality obligations arising from their employment relationship remain applicable to employees.[67]

70. If the agreement does not provide for the obligation of confidentiality, and decisions are considered which are likely to entail significant changes in work

65. Article 11.3 WEOR.
66. Article 11.4 WEOR.
67. Article 11.7 WEOR.

organisation or contractual relations, the consultation of employees and their representatives in the European and national employee participation bodies will start as simultaneously as possible.[68]

71. The central management has no obligation to provide information which would plausibly cause serious harm to or be prejudicial to the functioning of the Community-scale undertaking or group. Apart from the provisions listed above, parties are free to arrange the manner in which European participation takes shape. It goes without saying that the arrangements included in the agreement are to be complied with by all parties.

III. Termination, Expiring and Renegotiation

72. The WEOR formulates that an agreement shall contain provisions on the date of entry into force and the duration of the agreement. Likewise, it must include details about how it can be terminated or changed, as well as how it will deal with an increase or decrease in the number of employees within the undertaking or group. Just so, it must be determined how to deal with drastic changes in the structure of the Community-scale undertaking or group. In recent years, the Dutch court judged in one case, which dealt with a termination initiated by the central management. The existing EWC considered the termination to be a breach of contract.[69]

73. If the provisions in the agreement do not specify that employees (or their representatives) of undertakings or establishments joining the Community-scale undertaking or group after the conclusion of the agreement shall be involved within two years in the replacement or amendment thereof, or shall be represented in the EWC or the alternative information and consultation procedure within two years, the central management shall be obliged to set up a new special negotiating body if at least 100 such employees or their representatives so request.[70]

74. Procedures that lead to a termination of the agreement are provided by the agreement itself. There is neither a notice period prescribed that must be complied

68. Article 11.8 WEOR.
69. The Enterprise Chamber of the Amsterdam Court of Appeals ruled in 2004 in a situation, where the concerned EWC had been established under Belgian law. Following a merger, it was alleged that the EWC was no longer representative and the employer terminated the agreement. The Enterprise Chamber observed that the termination took place in compliance with the six-month notice period stipulated in the agreement. Besides, preparations were being made for the establishment of an EWC at the level of the parent undertaking. There was no legally enforceable obligation to maintain or establish an EWC at a subsidiary level, even if this was agreed beforehand. Enterprise Chamber, Amsterdam Court of Appeals, 1 January 2004, JOR 2004/134.
70. Article 11.6 WEOR.

with nor a procedure that must be followed (for instance, holding preliminary consultations). Relevant is that an EWC or alternative arrangement will continue to exist following the termination, to the extent that it relates to following a procedure that is connected to the termination.[71]

75. Special attention has been given to corporate restructurings (*see also* paragraph 43 beyond). The legislator ruled that, whenever an agreement must be altered as a result of a structural change, a new negotiation obligation arises, and another three-year period applies. The former EWC shall remain in force until a new council has been established. The legislator aimed to keep the information and consultation rights upright in turbulent times. Parties have the possibility to elaborate this further in the agreement. The members of the existing EWC will be involved in the negotiations, along with elected SNB members. The normal negotiation procedure applies, with an SNB supplemented by three members of the existing EWC (or three members for each EWC in case more EWCs are involved).[72] Independent from the termination or validity provisions, the existing agreements repeal once a new agreement comes into effect.

§2. The EWC According to the Subsidiary Requirements

76. The WEOR formulates the subsidiary provisions governing the provision of information and consultation in the absence of an agreement as an integral part of the Act. The legislator is well aware of the fact that these provisions might serve as a reference in the negotiations although negotiated agreements do not have to be subject to the detailed subsidiary requirements. In addition, the legislator has ruled that the general provisions with regard to the information and consultation procedures (Chapter 1 of the WEOR) have to be applied in all cases (both negotiated agreements and agreements based on the subsidiary requirements).[73]

I. Applicability and Enforcement of the Subsidiary Requirements

77. The subsidiary requirements make the establishment of an EWC mandatory and determine on which matters the employee representatives are informed and consulted. First of all, it has to be said that parties can agree to integrally apply the subsidiary requirements as the basic frame for an agreement. Furthermore, the central management is obliged to apply the subsidiary requirements, to organise the composition of the council and to call for a first meeting if:

71. Amsterdam district court 23 January 2003, JOR 2003/104.
72. Article 14a WEOR specifies this procedure. The article is based on Art. 13 EWC Recast Directive, which defines situations that require renegotiations. In the MVT 2011, the Dutch legislator mentions ‘mergers, takeovers or division of undertakings’. The legislator’s preference is that this is settled in the ordinary agreement. If this is not the case or contradicting relevant agreements are at stake, Art. 14a WEOR applies.
73. MVT 2011.

(a) there are indications that the central management will not enter into negotiations with a special negotiating body within six months of the receipt of a request to set up an SNB;
(b) the central management and the SNB have not concluded an agreement within three years after the receipt of a request or, if the central management has established a special negotiating body of its own accord, within three years of its doing so.[74]

II. Composition of the EWC

78. In the absence of an agreement, the composition of an EWC, installed on the basis of the subsidiary provisions, has to be in accordance with the prescribed composition of an SNB. This means that the number of employee representatives from the Community-scale undertaking or group of undertakings ensures that, in respect of each involved State, one member shall be elected or appointed, pursuant to the law of the Involved State in which he or she works, for each portion of employees employed in that State amounting to 10%, or a fraction thereof, of the number of employees working in all the involved States taken together. The WEOR also provides a mechanism for changes in the number of members.[75]

79. For Dutch members of the EWC, this means that membership should be in line with the notion of employees and with the regulation stipulated by the Dutch Works Councils Act.[76] The WEOR prescribes that only employees working for the Community-scale undertaking or group can become EWC members. Membership ends automatically when a member ceases to be an employee.[77] The term of office of members of an EWC, based on the subsidiary requirements, is four years.

80. The aim is to ensure optimal proportional representation of the various categories of employees. Thus, the division of the seats will have to be geared as much as possible to the various business activities within the undertaking, the employee categories and gender.[78]

III. Internal Organisation, Select Committee

81. The EWC elects a chairperson and one or more deputy chairpersons among its members. The chairperson, or if he is not available, the deputy chairperson, shall

74. Article 15.1 WEOR.
75. Article 16.1–16.3 WEOR.
76. Parliamentary Papers II 24.615, no. 3, p. 21.
77. Article 17.1 and 17.2 WEOR.
78. Parliamentary Papers II 2010/11, 32 705, no. 3, p. 17.

represent the EWC in law. The EWC formulates and adopts its own rules of procedure, after having given the central management the opportunity to give its view. The rules of procedures concern the internal working methods and do not bind others.[79]

82. Furthermore, the EWC can decide freely to elect among its members a select committee consisting of a maximum of five members. If a select committee is elected, the competences of that committee shall be set out in the rules of procedure, which shall also establish the resources necessary to enable it to pursue its activities.[80] EWC competences can be transferred to the committee. In practice, such a committee will often act as a management board or enlarged secretariat.

IV. Facilities, Resources, Costs

83. Expenses reasonably necessary for the EWC and the select committee to exercise their functions shall be borne by the Community-scale undertaking or the controlling undertaking. This also applies to the costs incurred in legal proceedings (such as attorney fees or court costs), but only under the condition that the Community-scale undertaking or the controlling undertaking has been notified in advance of the expense involved.[81] Unsuccessful proceedings are also eligible for reimbursement (provided they are not thought completely hopeless from the start).[82]

V. Meetings with the Central Management

84. The EWC will be given the opportunity to meet with the central management at least once a calendar year. The EWC shall be informed and consulted at such meeting, on the basis of a written report drawn up by the central management, on the progress of the business of the Community-scale undertaking or Community-scale group of undertakings and its prospects. These annual meetings are chaired alternately by the central management and the EWC, if no other arrangement is settled. The EWC or the select committee have the opportunity to meet before and after each meeting with the central management.[83]

---

79. Article 18.1 WEOR.
80. Article 18.2 and 18.3 WEOR.
81. Article 20.1 and 20.3 WEOR. For instance, the Enterprise Chamber ruled that the costs connected to a dispute about the question whether a European works council still existed after ending the agreement were eligible for reimbursement by the undertaking.
82. This is in conformity to the Dutch Works Councils Act, *see* Art. 22 WOR.
83. Article 19.4, 19.7 and 19.8 WEOR. The Dutch legislator added the notion of a ‘written report’.

VI. Competences of the EWC

85. The EWC may invoke information and consultation rights. Information should be given at such a time and in such a way that the employees' representatives can undertake an in-depth assessment of the consequences and may properly prepare any advice or comment.

86. The information that has to be supplied concerns:

(a) the structure, the economic and financial situation, the probable development of the activities, the production and sales of the Community-scale undertaking or group;
(b) the state and the probable development of employment, the investments, fundamental organisational changes, the implementation of new working methods or production processes, the care for the environment, mergers, or cutbacks of undertakings, branches or important divisions.

87. The central management has to inform the EWC (or the select committee) as quickly as possible about any exceptional circumstances or planned decisions which seriously affect the interests of the employees, particularly with respect to the relocation or closure of undertakings, establishments or significant parts thereof, or collective redundancies.[84] This obligation applies first and foremost to the central management of the Community-scale parent undertaking or group rather than to every local undertaking separately.[85]

88. Consultation of the EWC has to take place in case of 'cross-border issues'. This consultation is aimed at conducting a dialogue and exchanging points of view on the proposed measures. The aim is that the results of this dialogue can be considered when a decision is taken. Consultation should, therefore, take place at such time, in such fashion and with such content enabling employees' representatives to express an opinion on the basis of the information provided about proposed measures, and to obtain a reasoned response to the opinions they express.[86]

89. Cross-border issues are issues that are relevant to the entire Community-scale undertaking or group or to at least two undertakings or branches in two different Member States. During an advisory procedure, at least one consultation with the central management must take place. The guiding factor is the (positive and/or negative) impact of the decision on the organisation, rather than the number of countries involved.[87]

---

84. Article 19.1 and 19.2 WEOR.
85. European Court of Justice 15 June 2004, C-349/01, JOR 2004/267. *See also* European Court of Justice, 29 March 2001, C62/99, JOR 2001/143.
86. Article 1.1.h and Art. 17.3 of the WEOR.
87. Parliamentary Papers II 32.705, no. 3, pp. 13–14.

VII. Significant Structural Changes

90. The EWC may request to meet for extraordinary consultation purposes related to exceptional circumstances or planned decisions which seriously affect the interests of the employees. If the EWC or the select committee so requests, it shall meet the central management, or any other more appropriate level of management within the Community-scale undertaking or group, so as to be informed and consulted on the basis of a written report drawn up by the central management and relating to the circumstances or decisions referred to in the second subsection. The members of the EWC who are also elected or appointed by the employees of the establishments or undertakings directly affected by the circumstances or decisions concerned shall also be invited to attend a meeting with the select committee.[88]

VIII. Experts, Trade Unions and Employers' Associations

91. EWC and the select committee may be assisted by experts of their choice insofar as this is necessary for the performance of their duties. The obligation to bear the costs of the experts called in by the EWC shall be limited to one expert per agenda item, unless the EWC and the Community-scale undertaking or the controlling undertaking agree otherwise.[89] The WEOR does not refer in the subsidiary requirements to any role of trade unions and employers' organisations.

IX. Confidentiality

92. The provisions related to confidentiality are to a great extent similar to the confidentiality clause that applies to SNB members. In principle, the central management must supply the EWC with all information. However, if this information can reasonably be assumed to seriously impede or damage the functioning of the Community-scale undertaking or group, it need not be supplied. Alternatively, the central management may supply the information, while imposing a confidentiality obligation on the EWC members. In that case the central management must divulge which information is confidential, for how long the obligation of confidentiality obtains and with respect to which persons it need not be observed. This confidentiality obligation may also be imposed on council experts. Likewise, the confidentiality obligation may obtain for non-employees, such as union representatives.[90]

93. The duty of confidentiality does not cease upon the termination of a person's function in procedures in Community-scale undertakings and Community-scale groups of undertakings for the purposes of informing and consulting employees.[91]

88. Article 19.2 and 19.8 WEOR.
89. Article 20.1 and 20.2 WEOR.
90. Article 4.4 WEOR.
91. Article 4.6 WEOR.

X. Renegotiation

94. The legislator has included a clause that provides the EWC with the possibility to initiate negotiations for an agreement that is no longer ruled by the subsidiary requirements. At the latest, four years after being established on the basis of the subsidiary provisions, the EWC shall decide, in response to a proposal from the central management or otherwise, whether it is desirable to enter into negotiations with the central management on concluding a voluntary agreement. If this leads to negotiations, the EWC will replace the SNB, in accordance with all other obligations that are prescribed in the WEOR for negotiated agreements.[92]

§3. Status of Employees' Representativeness

95. The employees' representatives are facilitated and protected by the legislator. The personal rights and obligations that can be derived from the WEOR apply to any representation in the frame of the EWC, whether it be in a Dutch transnational or in an undertaking with its main seat outside the Netherlands. This application is also not restricted to members of the EWC. Article 4 of the WEOR guarantees EWC members, SNB members and other employee representatives that are active in procedures in any Community-scale undertaking and Community-scale group of undertakings for the purposes of informing and consulting employees facilities, insofar as is reasonably necessary for the exercise of their duties. However, these rights can only be derived by employee representatives working in the Netherlands.[93]

I. Working Time, Wage, Training and Facilities

96. Employees shall retain their entitlement to payment for the period of absence from work necessary to attend a meeting of the special negotiating body or the EWC or under the alternative information and consultation arrangements. This means, in practice, that employee representatives retain their entitlement to salary during the time they carry out duties in the interest of the EWC (or the SNB). Moreover, they shall be afforded the possibility – during working hours and without loss of pay – of taking part in mutual consultations and deliberations with other persons on matters concerning the performance of their duties.[94]

97. Employee representatives shall also be afforded the possibility – during working hours and without loss of pay – of taking part in education and training. They are entitled to other provisions they may reasonably be considered to need to fulfil their duty, such as the use of digital resources.

92. Article 21.1 and 21.2 WEOR.
93. Article 4.1 WEOR.
94. Article 4.2 and 4.3 WEOR.

98. In practice, most of the Dutch EWC members will cumulate facilities and protecting measures that can be derived from different representative functions. The key role of the national works council in the election and/or appointment of EWC members will often lead to cumulated mandates. The WEOR does not put limits to an accumulation of rights.

II. Legal Protection

99. The WEOR protects employee representatives from unfair treatment; this protection applies to candidate members and continues to apply once the membership of the EWC or SNB has ended: persons standing, or who have stood, as candidates for a function in procedures in Community-scale undertakings and Community-scale groups of undertakings for the purposes of informing and consulting employees, as well as those exercising or having exercised such a function, shall not suffer any disadvantage in their position within the undertaking for that reason.[95] Nevertheless, as, for instance, the confidentiality obligation follows directly from the employment relationship, disregard of the confidentiality obligation can result in sanctions under labour law, such as dismissal with immediate effect.

100. It is possible to bring these issues before the cantonal judge. This is a judge who is qualified to make a decision regarding a labour dispute. For instance, an employee may hold that he is placed in a disadvantageous position due to his or her membership of the special negotiating body, the EWC or his candidate membership. Or the employee may hold that he has not been paid his or her wages. This decision, however, will always be in conformity with the national law that applies to the employment relation.

101. First, a dismissal of employee representatives can only take place in accordance with the current ordinary dismissal system. Second, if an employer proceeds to terminate the employment agreement of an employee representative, a prohibition on termination has to be applied. The judge who has to rule about the termination request must decide whether the termination is connected to a prohibition on termination. This prohibition has a so-called extended scope of application.

102. In order to protect the legal status of an employee who is involved in EWC activities, the Dutch Civil Code prescribes that a worker's employment agreement may not be terminated if that worker:

(a) Is a member of an EWC.
(b) Has been placed on the list of candidates for an EWC.
(c) Has been a member of an EWC less than two years ago.

95. Article 4.7 WEOR.

(d) Has acted as a representative with a different form of information provision and consultation of employees set out in the WEOR less than two years ago.[96]

103. The Civil Code prescribes thus that a prohibition on termination continues to apply for two more years after an employee has been an EWC member or has acted as a representative with a different form of information provision and consultation of employees set out in the WEOR less than two years ago. The prolonged prohibition should prevent that the employer can proceed with dismissal due to the participatory activities of that employee when the term of office of an employee who is an EWC member expires. A prohibition on termination only for active members would only put off the evil and could hinder the works council members from acting independently.[97]

104. Legal protection of candidates for an EWC has been raised before the court. The procedure to be followed regarding the nomination of candidates is set out in the Dutch Work Councils Act.[98] The Arnhem district court has ruled in a case that an employee is a candidate from the moment the list of candidates has been submitted until the moment that the (new) works council members have been elected. The key question in this case was at what time an employee can be considered to be 'officially' placed on the list of candidates for an EWC.[99]

105. In line with case law on national election of representatives, the employee is also protected if any time passes between the moment when he or she has been elected and the moment when that employee actually takes up his or her duties as a member.[100] This means that an employee who has been placed on a list of candidates that has been submitted in conformity with the WOR procedure enjoys protection from dismissal at least until the moment when the EWC members are elected. If the candidate is actually elected, the employee enjoys protection from dismissal from the moment of election until the moment when he or she actually takes up his or her membership duties.[101]

106. In Part I Chapter 3 III §6, it was already mentioned that the Dutch legislator has essentially assigned employee representatives legal recourse to the Enterprise Chamber, which forms part of the Amsterdam Court of Appeal, for questions related to confidentiality and insufficient provision of information.[102]

---

96. Article 7:670 para. 4 and para. 10 Dutch Civil Code.
97. HR 31 March 2000, ECLI:NL:HR:2000:AA5319.
98. Article 9 WOR.
99. Arnhem district court, 4 November 1981, NJ 1982, 368.
100. Cantonal Court, Venlo. 2 December 1981, Prg. 1982, 1732.
101. WHWOR 1979, bill 13 954, Parliamentary Papers II, no. 6, p. 28 (MvA). Drongelen, J. van, Fase, W.J.P.M., and S.F.H. Jellinghaus, Individueel arbeidsrecht: Ontslagrecht, Uitgeverij Paris: Zutphen 2017, pp. 227–229.
102. Contrary to common usage, the Enterprise Chamber consists of five judges, two of whom are not jurists. These so-called laypersons usually have financial or economic backgrounds, such as accountancy.

III. Relationship Between EWC and Local Employees' Representatives

107. The WEOR prescribes that members of an EWC or representatives under any other procedure for informing and consulting employees shall inform the employee representatives within the Community-scale undertaking or group of undertakings or, if these do not exist, all the employees about the content and results of the information and consultation procedure carried out under the Act. However, the WEOR does not provide any enforcement mechanism of this obligation.

108. In the same article, the WEOR states that any confidentiality obligation cannot restrain the representative from informing the national works council or the employees' representatives about the substance and results of the information and consultation procedures.[103]

103. Article 4.8 WEOR.

Chapter 5. Pre-existing Agreements

109. The implementation of the EWC Directives had to take into account the existence of earlier concluded agreements. The legislator has elaborated a transitional legal frame that determines the (non-)applicability of the WEOR provisions.[104] Therefore, the WEOR prescribes two transitional arrangements for agreements that existed already before the entry into force of the Act of 7 November 2011 in conjunction with the implementation of EWC Recast Directive. This concerns, first, pre-existing agreements within the meaning of Article 13 of the EWC Directive and, second, negotiated agreements concluded under the original WEOR 1997.[105]

110. The first type of exemption, the continuation of pre-existing voluntary agreements, is certainly of relevance for EWC agreements under Dutch law. Some of the largest Dutch (and European) transnational companies concluded voluntary agreements (shortly) before the transposition deadline in 1996. For such pre-existing agreements within the meaning of Article 13 of the EWC Directive (later on confirmed in Article 14.1 of the EWC Recast Directive), it is stated that the WEOR shall not apply. This means that any Community-scale undertaking or group of undertakings, which was a party to one or more agreements which entered into force before 5 February 1997 (the date of the Dutch transposition of the EWC Directive entering into force), is exempted from applying the provisions of the new Act.

111. This exception applies mutatis mutandis to a Community-scale undertaking or group of undertakings, which as of 15 December 1999 would fall under the application of the WEOR on account solely of the entry into force of the Directive in the UK, but was at that date already a party to one or more agreements that had come into effect.[106]

112. However, the exception is conditionally formulated. The agreement should entail provisions for information and consultation of employees regarding cross-border issues and must have been concluded with employee representatives whom the Community-scale undertaking or group of undertakings could reasonably consider representative of the employees in the Involved States.

113. The second transitional provision was formulated by the Dutch legislator for agreements that were negotiated in the frame of the original WEOR 1997. This Act, as applicable on the day before the entry into force of the WEOR 2011, shall remain applicable to a Community-scale undertaking or group of undertakings which is a party to a negotiated agreement, relating to the entire workforce, and

104. In the MVT 2011, the Dutch legislator refers to a desire of the European Social Partners to take into account two different situations, in relation to earlier agreements.
105. Article 24 WEOR.
106. Article 24.1 and 24.4 WEOR.

which was signed or revised in the period from 5 June 2009 to 5 June 2011.[107] Moreover, it is still possible to revise and prolong agreements that were concluded under the original WEOR 1997, provided that this was explicitly intended and agreed before the entrance date of the new WEOR.

114. All exempted agreements, pre-existing agreements concluded prior to 5 February 1997 and those negotiated under the WEOR 1997, have to respect the articles in the newest consolidated WEOR regarding significant structural changes. The adaptation of agreements to significant structural changes is mandatory to all EWC Agreements (voluntary and negotiated, before and after transposition deadlines) and will lead to negotiations (*see* Chapter 3 of this monograph).[108]

115. Finally, any interested person who doubts that an exempted agreement fulfils the necessary conditions may request the Enterprise Chamber of the Amsterdam Court of Appeal to order implementation of the WEOR, i.e., the establishment of an agreement through negotiations (or a fallback on the subsidiary requirements).[109]

107. Article 24.2 WEOR.
108. Article 14a WEOR.
109. Article 5.1 WEOR.

Chapter 6. Coverage, Compliance and Enforcement

116. The coverage rate in the Netherlands is not substantially different from the rate in other Member States (*see* for updated data, *Part IV. Selected Agreements – a. Introductory remarks, facts and figures*). This is surprising for many observers, given the long tradition of national information, consultation and co-decision practices. On the other hand, the participation of Dutch members in EWCs established all over Europe is high, a clear substantiation of the country's open economy.

117. Findings of academic research regarding the absence of EWCs particularly in the Netherlands and in Germany (with a low take-up rate of 27%), as quoted by the European Commission during the preparations of the Recast Directive, pinpoint several reasons for this, mostly related to the perception that EWCs have limited added value.[110]

118. In the case of the Netherlands, it has to be mentioned that the central employers' organisation VNO-NCW opposed in its policy the adoption of the original EWC Directive until the very last moment. The organisation was a prominent opponent of the Directive in the ranks of the Union des Industries de la Communauté européenne (UNICE, now BusinessEurope) and demonstrated a hostile attitude to the introduction of information and consultation rights at European level as the EWC Directive was drafted.[111] VNO-NCW was of the opinion that enhanced rights would lead to delays in decision-making and repeated this position as the recast of the Directive was discussed.[112]

119. Another important reason is the absence of initiatives on the part of home-country worker representatives that might stem from a lack of interest. National works councils (and in larger Dutch-based firms, central works councils) have, in general, an easy access to the central management of undertakings. Works council members and the representative bodies at Dutch headquarters have enhanced national rights that guarantee proper information and consultation by central management. This phenomenon might influence the sense of urgency, certainly in cases where this relatively comfortable position is combined with a lack of knowledge regarding EWCs or with the opinion that EWCs are too weak to bring any benefit. Besides, in the view of national works councils the work of EWCs may interfere with the powers of national bodies or jeopardise home-country cooperative industrial relations. In practice, it can be very complicated and cumbersome for worker representatives in subsidiaries to take the necessary steps towards the creation of an EWC without the active support of the home-based representatives.

---

110. This is signalled in the Impact Assessment of the European Commission, 2008, Commission staff working document, Brussels, 2.7.2008, SEC(2008) 2166.
111. At https://www.nrc.nl/nieuws/1991/01/05/europese-or-schrikbeeld-voor-multinationals-6952045-a1137525, https://www.volkskrant.nl/archief/nederlandse-bedrijven-mijden-europese-or~a395281/.
112. At https://vno-ncw.nl/forum/de-tegenspraak-van-jan-cremers-pvda-%C2%91meer-inspraak-voor-europese-ondernemingsraad%C2%92.

120. The Dutch legislator has not chosen to enforce the observance of WEOR, and particularly the obligation to establish an EWC, by means of criminal or statutory sanctions. Basically, it is up to employers, employees and their representatives (unions and works councils) to ensure that the legal obligations are complied with. Central management shall start with procedures as soon as the management has received a written request to this end from at least 100 employees or their representatives in at least two undertakings or establishments in at least two different involved countries. If an undertaking fails to comply with the obligation to establish an EWC, a judge can institute civil proceedings to force the undertaking to comply with this legal obligation. Apart from that, there is still the option that an undertaking will establish an EWC on a voluntary basis.

121. Thus, enforcement of the WEOR is a matter of private law. The legislator has created the possibility for any stakeholder to file a petition with the Enterprise Chamber requesting it to impose compliance. This petition must be filed by a lawyer. The law stipulates that any stakeholder can request the judge to lay down that the legal or agreed-upon arrangements must be complied with. During the preparations of the WEOR, it became clear that this stakeholder notion can be broadly interpreted.[113] A petition can be filed by any stakeholder, such as employees, trade union or national works council.[114] The judge may impose a penalty payment in case of non-observance of his or her decision.[115]

122. The implementation of the EWC Recast Directive has neither introduced a change of the legal situation nor adaptations to the prevailing enforcement and sanctioning mechanism. Although the EWC Recast Directive introduces in its Consideration 36 the need to have sanctions that are effective, proportionate and dissuasive in cases of non-compliance, the Dutch legislator stated that it was not necessary to change the WEOR in this respect. This was argued with reference to the general statement in one article already included in the WEOR 1997 (Article 5.1). This article provides any interested person with the possibility to request the Enterprise Chamber of the Amsterdam Court of Appeal to order implementation of the provisions of the WEOR. This Enterprise Chamber has the competence to order the implementation of the Directive (with fines) or to arbitrate about its existence.[116]

123. In general, the Enterprise Chamber has not been confronted with many cases. The Chamber has, in its very first EWC case in April 2004, ruled that the Dutch telecommunications company Equant NV did not act unlawfully when it terminated the 1997 agreement establishing the Global One European Employee Forum (EEF) following Global One's merger with Equant in 2001. Equant, which is part of the France Telecom group, informed its European Forum in 2002 about the intention to terminate the agreement. The ideas were to initiate negotiations to set up an EWC at the level of Equant. The members of the Forum considered the

---

113. Parliamentary Papers 24.641, no. 3, p. 23 j° pp. 12–13.
114. Article 5 WEOR.
115. Parliamentary Papers 24.641, no. 6, p. 13.
116. *Memorie van toelichting* (MVT 2011), page 13.

continuation of the Forum activities until a new agreement was concluded, but this was rejected by the company. France Telecom decided against having an EWC specifically covering Equant. The court ruled that Equant was entitled to terminate the agreement establishing the Forum. The firm had respected the notice period and could not be forced to establish an Equant EWC because France Telecom, not Equant, constituted the group's controlling undertaking.[117]

124. Scholars have pinpointed that the Dutch legislator introduced with the implementation of the EWC Recast Directive a change of direction in this respect. The current WEOR says in Article 14a that in case of major restructurings an existing EWC(s) or another procedure for informing and consulting workers shall apply and function in accordance with the applicable agreement or agreements during the negotiations.

117. Holtzer, M. (2014). De invloed van werknemers op de strategie van de vennootschap, University of Groningen, https://www.rug.nl/research/portal/files/10904305/Thesis_Holtzer.pdf.

Chapter 7. Implementation of Directive 2009/38/EC (the 'Recast')

125. Article 15 of the EWC Directive (94/45/EC) prescribes a review of the functioning of the Directive 'Not later than 22 September 1999'. The European Commission 'shall, in consultation with the Member States and with management and labour at European level, review its operation and, in particular examine whether the workforce size thresholds are appropriate with a view to proposing suitable amendments to the Council, where necessary'.[118]

126. The revision of the EWC Directive that led to Directive 2009/38/EC (hereinafter, 'the EWC Recast Directive') has been the result of a long consultative and legislative process that started that at the beginning of the new millennium. The outcome is based on the assessments from the European Commission, a joint advice of the European social partners and several position papers of the European Parliament.[119] The EWC Recast Directive aims, next to an improvement of competences with better definitions and enhanced facilities, to promote the compliance with the obligation to transpose the directive. The input for a better functioning of EWCs went in two directions:

(1) the principle of information and consultation at a time and with a content that allows the EWC members an in-depth assessment in order to formulate an opinion on the envisaged measures;
(2) the broadening up of different aspects of assistance and of means (to mention more regular meetings, the right to extraordinary meetings and follow-up, but also steering, experts and training).

127. The Dutch legislator implemented the EWC Recast Directive with an Act (Act of 7 November 2011) that combined several unchanged provisions of the existing European Works Councils Act (WEOR) with a series of amendments.[120] The

118. Article 15, *Council Directive 94/45/EC of 22 September 1994 on the establishment of a European Works Council or a procedure in Community-scale undertakings and Community-scale groups of undertakings for the purposes of informing and consulting employees*. http://eur-lex.europa.eu/legal-content/EN/TXT/PDF/?uri=CELEX:31994L0045&from=EN visited 24 Aug. 2017.
119. The European Parliament was one of the driven forces for a revision. After a first report from the Commission (COM/2000/188 final) with no clear timing of a possible revision, the EP stated that the actual coverage was unsatisfactory and that there were too many gaps on workers' rights to information and consultation. The EP urged the Commission to submit a proposal for the revision of Directive 94/45/EC in its report of 16 July 2001 (A5-0282/2001 final). The EP repeated this request in 2006 and 2007 in resolutions. As the Commission initiated the legislative process in 2007/2008 through a formal Social Dialogue consultation, the social partners could not reach a final joint position. Consequently, the Commission tabled its proposals. The French presidency invited the social partners to react on the proposals. The resulting Joint Advice (29 Aug. 2008) was seen as a strong recommendation. The European Parliament and the Council adopted in a first reading the EP's report (16 Dec. 2008). On 23 Apr. 2009, the Council adopted the revised directive on European Works Councils (the Recast Directive).
120. The initial EU Directive (94/45/EC) was transposed in 1997. Later on, the Dutch legislator two times slightly modified the Act, as a consequence of the UK application Directive (97/74/EC) and the Directive that settles the accession of Bulgaria and Romania (2006/109/EC).

legislator repealed the WEOR 1997 and kept the same name for the new Act. The legal base was not changed, compared to the WEOR 1997.

128. With the argument that the drafting of the EWC Recast Directive was strongly influenced by the European social partners, the Dutch legislator decided to consult the social partners that regularly meet in their joint Foundation of Labour. The government's request for advice on the implementation led to an advice of the social partners on 6 December 2010.[121] The Foundation formulated a series of comments on the draft and some editorial changes. The social partners, gathered in the Foundation, stressed the need to follow as close as possible the text of the EWC Recast Directive.

129. Furthermore, the Foundation's advice underlined that the Dutch legislator should determine how the selection (election/nomination) of the Dutch members of an EWC has to take place. For the Foundation, this is a pre-condition for keeping upright the character of the Dutch 'co-decision' tradition. The different comments led to editorial changes and clarifications. The MVT 2011 of the national transposition underlines the important communication function of the EWC for the company management. Workers' involvement is necessary in decision-making processes as it can increase commitment. Proper consultation contributes to the 'social cohesion' inside a company.

130. The final transposition corresponds broadly with the general text of the EWC Recast Directive. However, there are several (minor) stipulations that tighten up the provisions of the EWC Recast Directive:

- Some procedural aspects of Annex 1 of the EWC Recast Directive (the subsidiary requirements) are more clearly prescribed in paragraph 3 of the WEOR (the subsidiary provisions governing the provisions of information and consultation in the absence of an agreement). The Dutch legislator has specified that the EWC shall be informed and consulted before the annual meeting, on the basis of a *written* report drawn up by the central management, on the progress of the business of the Community-scale undertaking or Community-scale group of undertakings and its prospects.
- Also some facilities that were not specified in detail in the subsidiary requirements of the EWC Recast Directive were materialised, for instance, the right of the EWC to gather on its own, before and after the meeting with the central management without the latter being present, and the chair of the meetings has to rotate between management and labour, unless otherwise agreed.
- The funding of several provisions is guaranteed, i.e., the financing of the training by the employer is explicitly regulated in the subsidiary provisions and the management is obliged to bear the costs of the experts called in by the EWC. This is limited to one expert per agenda item, unless the EWC and the Community-scale undertaking or the controlling undertaking agree otherwise.

---

121. At https://www.stvda.nl/~/media/Files/Stvda/Nota/2010_2019/2010/20101206/20101206.ashx.

Part II. The Act on European Works Councils and the Recast Situated in the National Juridical Frame

Chapter 1. The Dutch Works Council Act (WOR)

131. The legislator aimed to work out a transposition into national law of the EWC Directives that was consistent with the existing national legislation, notably with the Dutch Works Council Act (WOR). The WOR provides workers with information, consultation and co-decision rights in companies that are established in the Netherlands. It has to be taken into account that the more far-reaching notion of co-decision or co-determination has been enshrined in the Dutch constitution since 1983. Article 19.2 of the constitution says that 'Rules concerning the legal status and protection of working persons and concerning co-determination shall be laid down by Act of Parliament.'[122] In the Dutch industrial relations theory, these rights are seen as features of democratic provisions that guarantee a certain equilibrium of the power balance between management and labour at the company level.[123]

132. The scope of the WOR is limited to the Dutch territory, i.e., to the workforce that is active within companies that perform their activities in the Netherlands. Workers of companies, established in the Netherlands, who carry out work in another territory cannot derive rights from the WOR. The competence of WOR representatives is primarily bound to decisions that are taken by the board or management in the Netherlands. The EWC Directives have introduced a body of workers' representation at European level that provides workers with the complementary right to exert influence on decisions that are taken at European level. The WEOR contributes to a more effective functioning of the national councils in transnational companies. Relevant in this regard is also the implementation of Council Directive 2001/86/EC of 8 October 2001 supplementing the Statute for a European company with regard to the involvement of employees and of Council Directive 2003/72/EC of 22 July 2003 supplementing the Statute for a European Cooperative Society with regard to the involvement of employees (treated in Chapter 9).

122. At https://www.government.nl/documents/regulations/2012/10/18/the-constitution-of-the-kingdom-of-the-netherlands-2008.
123. Kaar, R., van het, E. Smit, W. Buitelaar (et al.) (2006) Vier scenario's voor de toekomst van de medezeggenschap, Eburon Delft.

133. As mentioned before, the legislator opted for a transposition in a separate act, not for the integration in the existing WOR. Scholars have argued that the main reason for the legislator was to stress that the EWC is not the 'ultimate' representative body. There is no aim to establish a hierarchy; information and consultation rights derived from EU law exist next to national legislation already in force. A second reason is that the notion of co-decision as situated and developed in the Dutch industrial relations provides the national works councils with far-reaching rights that go beyond the EWC rights. The separation emphasises the fact that these rights are left intact (or even sometimes prevail). A third reason is that several formulated rights are not identically defined in national and EU legislation.

134. The national work council and its members are explicitly mentioned in the WEOR. The most important aspect is the role that the national works council has to play in the appointment of representatives for the EWC. The national works council is the main reference for the appointment of the Dutch members of the SNB (Article 10 WEOR). And, in practice, the nomination of EWC members by the national works councils is the prevailing procedure once an EWC is established. Moreover, the WEOR refers in several articles to the role and functioning of members of a national works council. As mentioned before, Article 3 of the WEOR stipulates that 'employee representatives' means those persons defined as such under the law of the Involved State in which the employees are working. In the case of the Netherlands, it means members of the Dutch Works Councils. Members of Dutch Works Councils have the right to the necessary information before the opening of negotiations, the right to ask for negotiations and the right to be informed about the link between the information and consultation of the EWC and the information and consultation at the national level.

135. The WOR contains several principles and guidelines that are directly or indirectly relevant for the functioning of the WEOR.[124] For instance, the provision in the Dutch Works Council that consultation must take place at the level of management and representation appropriate to the subject to be discussed (Article 4.8.b) directly relates to the subsidiarity and the division of labour between a Dutch Works Council and an EWC. As said before, the election procedure formulated for members of the national works councils (who is eligible to vote, who is eligible to stand, who can nominate candidates and the term of office) determines in general also the composition of the group of workers representatives that can be appointed as member of an EWC. The consequence is that a member of the EWC who is also a national works council member can rely on the protection stemming from the WOR for his or her activities.

136. The competences listed in the Dutch WOR refer to several items that can be relevant for the activity of the EWC, such as consultation rights on decisions like transfer of undertakings, takeovers, major restructurings and termination of activities. Some of these competences are restricted or do not apply, for instance, in case

---

124. An English text of the WOR is available on the website of the Dutch Social and Economic Council SER: https://www.ser.nl/~/media/files/internet/talen/engels/2013/works-councils-act.ashx.

of takeovers if the other enterprise is established or is being established abroad. However, there are already 'best practices' of the use of these national rights in major events in a transnational company, combined with the more limited information and consultation rights at EU level.

137. In the area of information rights, prescribed by the WOR, it is worth mentioning that the company, including an entrepreneur forming part of an international group of enterprises, has to provide the members of the Dutch Works Council at the beginning of every term of office with written information about the enterprise (Article 31 WOR). In case the entrepreneur forms part of a group of entrepreneurs or maintains long-term relations with foreign entrepreneurs or organisations, this information also concerns the entrepreneurs forming the group, the power structures linking them and the names and addresses of those who in consequence of the said power structures are able to exercise actual control over the enterprise.

138. The Dutch WOR prescribes that the employer shall, at least twice a year, provide the works council, either orally or in writing, with general information concerning the activities and financial results of the enterprise (Article 31a). In case the employer belongs to a group of associated entrepreneurs and this financial information is included in a consolidated annual account as mentioned in Article 405 of Book 2 of the Dutch Civil Code, the employer shall submit to the works council for the purposes of discussion a copy of this consolidated annual account, the annual report and the other information as mentioned in Article 392 of the said Book regarding the legal body that compiled the consolidated annual account. This implies that information on foreign entities that are consolidated in the group has to be provided. Of course, this is only applicable in Dutch-based groups, but it gives information about transnational activities.

Chapter 2. Other Relevant Parts of the Acquis

139. Council Directive 2001/86/EC of 8 October 2001 supplementing the Statute for a European company with regard to the involvement of employees and Council Directive 2003/72/EC of 22 July 2003 supplementing the Statute for a European Cooperative Society with regard to the involvement of employees (hereinafter 'SE/SCE Statutes') were transposed into Dutch law in the Act on the role of employees in European Company Statutes of 17 March 2005. This Act lays down the demarcation between the EWC Directives and the workers' representation in the SE and SCE.[125]

140. The SE/SCE Act regulates that in Community-scale undertakings or controlling undertakings of a communitarian group with the SE Statute (in Article 1.6) or the SCE Statute (Article 2.6) the WEOR shall not apply to that undertaking and its subsidiaries, unless the SNB (of the SE/SCE) decides to refrain from negotiations or to cease ongoing negotiations. As a consequence, the WEOR serves as a fallback regulation in situations where workers' representatives in an SE or SCE are confronted with an impending lack of European information and consultation rights. Actually, the SE/SCE Act has led in five cases to the creation of an EWC (although the name might be different).[126]

141. A second relationship that was construed during the implementation of SE/SCE Statutes is of an indirect character. As has been mentioned before, an important legal provision was introduced in the slipstream of the implementation of the SE/SCE Directives. An amendment that led to a modification of the WEOR 1997 introduced the possibility for special negotiating bodies and EWCs to appeal to the Enterprise Chamber of the Amsterdam Court in well-defined cases, such as the removal of disproportionate confidentiality duties or the unreasonable refusal to provide the necessary information (actually, Article 5.2 WEOR).

142. A last area, which has to be mentioned briefly, is the relationship with information and consultation rights that can be derived from other parts of the EU Acquis, notably rights that have been formulated in the area of company law, such as the EU Takeover Bids Directive (2004/25/EC), the EU Directive on the Transfer of Undertakings (2001/23/EC) or the EU Directive on Cross-Border Mergers. The EU and national legislators have defined certain rights for workers and their representatives to information, consultation and participation in decision-making in such situations. The demarcation with existing rights is normally formulated in clauses stating that the Directive shall be without prejudice to existing national and EU rights on information, consultation and, if provided, co-determination. And, for instance, for the EU Takeover Bids Directive, it was found that the implementation of this Directive did not lead to new worker rights above and beyond what was

125. Another EU Directive, the 2002 EU information and consultation Directive (2002/14/EC) had no great impact in the Netherlands as the Dutch Works Councils Act already covered most of the issues raised by the Directive.
126. Recorded in www.ewcdb.eu (visited 15 Dec. 2017).

required in the Netherlands. Nevertheless, in such situations of major restructurings, the fine-tuning between the different levels and instruments for information and consultation is at stake.[127]

127. Cremers, J. and Vitols, S. 2016, Takeovers with or without worker voice: workers' rights under the EU Takeover Bids Directive, ETUI, Brussels.

Chapter 3. Impact and Complementary Effect

143. This monograph describes how the Dutch legislator has transposed the rules and provisions of the EWC Directives. The main aim was to complement the existing national legislation in this area. The legislator has endorsed the necessity of EU information and consultation rights. This position could all the more be substantiated with evidence stemming from research in the field of industrial relations and labour law. The Dutch co-decision is in danger of getting into a vacuum, with decision and policymaking being transferred to centres in undertakings that are no longer situated in the Dutch territory. The EU rights of information and consultation compensate this development (to a limited extent).

144. The Dutch transposition of the EWC Directives, based on a separate Act next to the WOR that grounds that national rights, underlines that there is no hierarchical relationship between both types of workers' rights. The separate Act also indicates that there is no equal footing between the two types of rights. The WEOR underpins (and is limited to) certain rights related to transnational issues. It should create favourable conditions for the functioning of (central) works councils of undertakings, which are part of transnational companies that fall within the scope of the EWC Directives.[128]

145. Through an EWC, the national representatives of transnational companies, both Dutch and foreign, have an entrance to the power centre of a company, with the possibility to gain more insight into the overall strategy, the future of the company and (other) corporate governance. The EWC provides additional means to participate in the preparation and implementation of transnational measures or decisions. It creates possibilities to discuss and influence the overall social policy and to reflect on convergence and divergence with colleagues from other involved undertakings. In that respect, the introduction of an EWC has brought an added value to the already existing national model of co-decision, information and consultation. Based on my own practice, it can be added that the positive effect for the central management of a company is that the EWC creates a non-hierarchical antennae for the ins and outs of a company.

146. One of the key questions, however, is how the (grown) rights derived from EU legislation fit in the existing instruments, for instance, how these rights can be matched to the extensive Dutch information and consultation rights and what is necessary to place foreign representatives on an equal footing. The bottleneck becomes in practice especially manifest in transnational decisions that involve the relocation of production and employment and that result in job losses and collective redundancies. In those situations, national representatives often can rely on information and

128. MVT 2011.

consultation rights that go far beyond the EWC provisions, with more frequent concertation talks than the EWC. Coordination among employee representatives is a key in these situations; the positive effect that mutual alignment will be stimulated.[129]

147. The national works council Act WOR provides a structure of works councils (also for the subsidiaries), group works councils (GORs) and central works councils (CORs) for complex companies and groups of undertakings. This asks for the necessary coordination between these employee participation bodies, which will become even more intensive if there is an EWC in the company. For national (central) works councils, the cooperation and coordination with the EWC, in particular through coordinated advice and consultation processes, is especially important in keeping grip on transnational decision-making.[130]

129. Beurden, P. van (et al.), 2009, Gebruik, niet-gebruik of onderbenutting? Onderzoek naar de mogelijke onderbenutting van bevoegdheden en mogelijkheden door de (Centrale) Ondernemingsraad in grote Nederlandse ondernemingen, pp. 33, 38, 39.

130. Heiden, P. van der (et al.), 2012, Medezeggenschap: Ontwikkelingen in de 21e eeuw, SER, The Hague.

Part III. The EWC Directive as Transposed into National Law[131]

a. EWC Act of 23 January 1997
b. EWC Act: Amendments of 7 November 2011
c. EWC Act of 7 November 2011: Consolidated Version

131. For the English text of the Act, the authors edited the unofficial English language translation, as published by the European Commission: http://ec.europa.eu/social/main.jsp?catId=707&langId=en&intPageId=211.

a. EWC Act of 23 January 1997

ACT OF 23 JANUARY 1997

for the implementation of Council Directive 94/45/EC of 22 September 1994 on the establishment of a European Works Council or a procedure in Community-scale undertakings and Community-scale groups of undertakings for the purposes of informing and consulting employees

(European Works Councils Act)

We Beatrix, by the grace of God Queen of the Netherlands, Princess of Orange-Nassau, etc. etc. etc.

Greetings to all who shall see or hear these presents! Be it known:

Whereas we have considered it necessary to implement Council Directive 94/45/EC of 22 September 1994 on the establishment of a European Works Council or a procedure in Community-scale undertakings and Community-scale groups of undertakings for the purposes of informing and consulting employees;

We, therefore, having heard the Council of State and in consultation with the States-General [Parliament], have approved and decreed as we hereby approve and decree:

Chapter 1.
General Provisions

Article 1

1. In this Act:

'Member State' means a Member State of the European Union or another State, which is party to the Agreement on the European Economic Area, except for the United Kingdom;
'Directive' means Council Directive 94/45/EC of 22 September 1994 on the establishment of a European Works Council or a procedure in Community-scale undertakings and Community-scale groups of undertakings for the purposes of informing and consulting employees (EC OJ L 254):
'Community-scale undertaking' means an undertaking, which for two years has had an average of at least 150 employees in at least two Member States and an average of at least 1,000 employees in the Member States taken together, unless it belongs to a Community-scale group;
'Community-scale group' means a combination of undertakings consisting of a controlling undertaking as referred to in Article 2 and an undertaking or undertakings over which it exercises control, in which:

1°. at least two undertakings are situated in different Member States, and
2°. for two years at least one undertaking has had an average of at least 150 employees in one Member State and another undertaking has had an average of at least 150 employees in another Member State, and
3°. all the undertakings taken together have for two years had an average of at least 1,000 employees in the Member States;

'Central management' means, in the case of a Community-scale undertaking, the management of such an undertaking, and in the case of a Community-scale group, the management of the controlling undertaking as referred to in Article 2.

2. Where the domicile or headquarters of a Community-scale undertaking is not situated in a Member State, the central management shall be deemed to be:
   a. a person appointed by the Community-scale undertaking and actually in charge of managing one of its establishments in a Member State, or failing that:
   b. the person or persons actually in charge of the establishment employing the greatest number of employees in any one Member State.
3. Where the domicile or headquarters of the controlling undertaking as referred to in Article 2 is not situated in a Member State, the controlling undertaking may designate as its representative the management of a group undertaking having its domicile or headquarters in a Member State. Failing such a designation, the management of the group undertaking which has its domicile or headquarters in a Member State and which employs the greatest number of employees in any one Member State will be deemed to be such.
4. Action or failure to take action by the central management as referred to in article 1, sub 1.e, respectively sub 3 shall be the responsibility of the natural or legal person maintaining the Community-scale undertaking or controlling undertaking or the group undertaking as referred to in article 3.

Article 2

1. In this Act, 'controlling undertaking' means the undertaking within a Community-scale group, which can directly or indirectly exercise a dominant influence over another undertaking and over which no other undertaking exercises a dominant influence directly or indirectly. Unless otherwise shown to be the case, an undertaking shall be presumed to be the controlling undertaking if it:
   a. can appoint more than half of the members of the other undertaking's administrative, management or supervisory body, or
   b. can exercise over half of the voting rights at the general meeting of that other undertaking, or
   c. holds over 50 % of another undertaking's subscribed capital.
2. For the purposes of Article 2, sub 1.a controlling undertaking's rights as regards capital, voting and appointment shall include:

   a. the corresponding rights of other undertakings over which it exercises a dominant influence;
   b. the corresponding rights of any person or body acting in his or its own name but for account of the controlling undertaking or of one or more of its group undertakings.
3. For the purposes of subsection 1, the rights concerning capital and voting shall not be attributed to an undertaking which holds them for account of others.
4. For the purposes of subsection 1, voting rights attached to pledged shares shall be attributed to the creditor if he is authorised to decide how these rights are to be exercised. However, if the shares have been pledged as collateral for a loan, which the creditor has provided in the usual course of his business, the voting rights shall only be attributed to him if he has exercised them on his own behalf.
5. No undertaking as referred to in article 3(5) at (a) or (c) of Council Regulation (EEC) No. 4064/89 of 21 December 1989 on the control of concentrations between undertakings[132](OJ L 395) shall be deemed to be a controlling undertaking.
6. The law applicable to an undertaking shall determine whether that undertaking is a controlling undertaking as referred to in subsection 1. If such law is not the law of a Member State, this matter shall be determined by the law applying to the group undertaking whose management represents the controlling undertaking pursuant to section 1(3).
7. If several undertakings within a group meet with one or more of the criteria laid down in subsection 1:
   a. the undertaking which satisfies the criterion laid down in point a. of that subsection shall be deemed to be the controlling undertaking, with the right of appointment regarding the management body taking priority;
   b. where point a. does not lead to an undertaking being deemed to be the controlling undertaking, the criterion laid down in point b. shall take priority over that set out in point c., without prejudice to proof that another undertaking is able to exercise a dominant influence.

---

132. *A concentration shall not be deemed to arise where:*

a) credit institutions or other financial institutions or insurance companies, the normal activities of which include transactions and dealing in securities for their own account or for the account of others, hold on a temporary basis securities which they have acquired in an undertaking with a view to reselling them, provided that they do not exercise voting rights in respect of those securities with a view to determining the competitive behaviour of that undertaking or provided that they exercise such voting rights only with a view to preparing the sale of all part of that undertaking or of its assets or the sale of those securities and that any such sale takes place within one year of the date of acquisition; that period may be extended by the Commission on request where such institutions or companies justify the fact that the sale was not reasonably possible within the period set; (...)

c) the operations (direct or indirect acquisition) carried out by the financial holding companies (...), provided however that the voting rights in respect of the holding are exercised, in particular in relation to the appointment of members of the management and supervisory bodies of the undertakings in which they have holdings, only to maintain the full value of those investments and not to determine directly or indirectly the competitive conduct of those undertakings.

Article 3

1. In this Act the term 'employees' means, insofar as persons working in the Netherlands are concerned, persons working under an employment contract in the Community-scale undertaking or the Community-scale group and, where it applies to persons working in other Member States, the persons defined as such under the law of the relevant Member State.
2. For the purposes of Articles 4(9), 7, 8(2), 11(6) and 19(7), 'employees' representatives' means those persons defined as such under the law of the Member State in which the employees are working; in the case of the Netherlands it means works councils.

Article 4

1. Subsections 2 to 8 shall apply to employees working in the Netherlands who are members of a special negotiating body or of a European Works Council or act as representatives under alternative arrangements for informing and consulting employees.
2. Such employees shall retain their entitlement to payment for the period of absence from work necessary to attend a meeting of the special negotiating body or the European Works Council or under the alternative information and consultation arrangements.
3. Insofar as is reasonably necessary for the exercise of their duties they shall be afforded the possibility – during working hours and without loss of pay – of taking part in mutual consultations and deliberations with other persons on matters concerning the performance of their duties, and of undergoing education and training.
4. They must maintain confidentiality on all business and company secrets which come to their knowledge in their capacity as representatives as well as on all matters designated confidential or whose confidential nature they ought to appreciate in the light of the confidentiality requirement imposed. This also applies to persons who are not employees but perform a function as referred to in subsection 1.
5. The duty of confidentiality shall not apply to anyone brought in for consultation or as an expert as referred to in Articles 12 and 20, provided that the central management or the person who has imposed the confidentiality requirement has given due approval beforehand and the person involved has declared in writing that he undertakes to observe confidentiality on the matter concerned. In such cases the duty of confidentiality shall apply to the person in question.
6. The duty of confidentiality shall not cease upon the termination of a person's function as referred to in subsection 1 or the termination of a person's employment at the undertaking.

7. The employer shall ensure that persons standing, or who have stood, as candidates for a function as referred to in subsection 1, as well as those exercising or having exercised such a function, shall not suffer any disadvantage in their position within the undertaking for that reason.
8. With regard to an employee exercising a function as referred to in subsection 1, or who exercised such a function less than two years ago respectively, section 21, subsections 2 or 3 and 4 to 6, of the Works Councils Act shall apply mutatis mutandis.
9. Any employee or employee representative working in the Netherlands may require the employer to notify him of the number of employees working in the Community-scale undertaking or group, as well as the distribution of such employees across the various Member States.
10. The employer of an employee working in the Netherlands and appointed or elected as a member of a special negotiating body or of a European Works Council shall report such appointment or election to the central management.

Article 5

Any interested person may request the Enterprise Chamber of the Amsterdam Court of Appeal to order implementation of the provisions of this Act, with the exception of Article 4, subsections 1 to 8, or of an agreement as referred to in Article 11 or 24. A special negotiating body or the members thereof and a European Works Council established under this Act may not be ordered to pay the costs of such proceedings. Articles 429a to 429t of the Code of Civil Procedure shall apply.

Chapter 2.
Informing and Consulting Employees in Dutch Community-Scale Undertakings and Groups

Paragraph 1

General Provisions

Article 6

1. This chapter shall apply to Community-scale undertakings and controlling undertakings with their domicile or headquarters in the Netherlands.
2. Where the domicile or headquarters of a Community-scale undertaking or controlling undertaking is not situated in a Member State, this chapter shall apply if the domicile or headquarters of the establishment or group undertaking as referred to in Article 1(2) and (3) is situated in the Netherlands.

Article 7

The Community-scale undertaking or controlling undertaking shall be obliged to state – at the request of employees or employees' representatives – the number of employees working in the Community-scale undertaking or Community-scale group, as well as the distribution of such employees across the various Member States.

Paragraph 2

Agreements on the Provisions of Information and Consultation

Article 8

1. The central management may set up a special negotiating body for the purpose of entering into negotiations with it concerning an agreement on establishing a European Works Council, whether or not in accordance with paragraph 3, or on making other arrangements for providing information to and consulting employees or their representatives on transnational matters.
2. The central management shall be obliged to set up a special negotiating body as referred to in subsection 1 if a written request to this end has been received from at least 100 employees or their representatives in at least two undertakings or establishments in at least two different Member States. If such a request is received by an establishment or undertaking belonging to a Community-scale undertaking or group, the central management shall ensure that the request is transmitted to it without delay and that the persons who made the request are informed of this.
3. Where the special negotiating body has taken a decision as referred to in Article 11(2), the obligation referred to in subsection 2 above shall not apply during the two years following the taking of such a decision, unless the central management and the special negotiating body have agreed otherwise.

Article 9

1. The special negotiating body shall consist of one member for each Member State in which employees of the Community-scale undertaking or group work and one, two or three supplementary members respectively for each Member State in which at least one quarter, one half or three-quarters of the employees work.
2. Each member shall be elected or appointed pursuant to the law of the Member State in which he works.
3. The allocation of the seats shall be kept in accordance with subsection 1; if this leads to a change in the number of supplementary members for a Member State without there having been a new election or appointment to fill such seats, the members holding office for that Member State shall, for the purposes of Article 13, together hold as many votes as the number of seats laid down for that Member State under subsection 1.

Article 10

1. With regard to Dutch establishments and undertakings, the members of the special negotiating body shall be appointed, or their appointment terminated, by the works councils set up at such establishments or undertakings.
2. If, in respect of works councils as referred to in subsection 1, one or more central works councils have been established, the said appointment or termination shall be effected by the latter council or councils.
3. If no central works council has been set up, but there are one or more group works councils, the said appointment or termination shall be effected by the latter council or councils.
4. If not all works councils or group works councils are represented in a central works council or group works council, the said appointment or termination shall be effected jointly by the central or group works council or councils and the non-represented works councils.
5. If no works council has been set up, the members of the special negotiating body shall be elected by the entire body of employees working in the Netherlands for the Community-scale undertaking or group. The election shall be by secret written ballot, each employee having one vote. An association of employees having aforementioned employees as its members, with a constitution defining its aim as promoting the interests of its members as employees, active in this manner within the undertaking or group involved and also enjoying full legal capacity, may present a list of candidates for the aforementioned election, provided that it has consulted its members within the undertaking or group on the composition of the list of candidates.
6. For the purposes of subsections 1 to 4, employees of Dutch establishments or undertakings who are not represented in a works council, group works council or central works council will be given the opportunity to express an opinion about the persons to be appointed as members of the special negotiating body.
7. Persons who are seafarers in the merchant navy shall not be appointed or elected as members of a special negotiating body.

Article 11

1. After the special negotiating body has been set up, the central management shall convene a meeting with it in order to negotiate an agreement as referred to in Article 8(1). It shall give the negotiating body the opportunity to meet prior to such a meeting.
2. As long as no agreement as referred to in Article 8(1) has been concluded, the special negotiating body may decide not to enter into negotiations or to terminate negotiations already in progress.
3. If the central management and the special negotiating body agree to set up a European Works Council, agreement shall also be reached on the Council's rules of procedure. Unless otherwise agreed by the central management and the special negotiating body, the rules of procedure shall at least regulate the following:

   a) the establishments or undertakings of the Community-scale undertaking or group for which the European Works Council is being set up;
   b) the size and composition of the European Works Council and its members' term of office;
   c) the Council's scope and competence;
   d) the arrangements for informing and consulting the Council;
   e) the frequency, duration and venue of Council meetings;
   f) the financial and material resources to be placed at the Council's disposal.
4. If the central management and the special negotiating body agree on a different information and consultation procedure for employees or their representatives not involving the establishment of a European Works Council, the corresponding arrangements shall also be laid down in an agreement. This must include at least the following:
   a) the establishments or undertakings of the Community-scale undertaking or group to which the procedure applies;
   b) the way in which the employees or their representatives are to be informed and consulted on transnational questions which significantly affect employees' interests;
   c) the manner in which employees or their representatives may meet to discuss the questions referred to in point b;
   d) the financial and material resources to be made available to implement the procedure.
5. The central management and the special negotiating body may agree to set up separate European Works Councils for different parts of the Community-scale undertaking or group, or to apply separate procedures. They may also agree to set up one or more European Works Councils for one or more parts of the Community-scale undertaking or group and introduce one or more procedures for other parts.
6. The agreement between the central management and the special negotiating body shall contain provisions governing the duration of the agreement and the arrangements for negotiating a new agreement and for adapting the agreement to changes in the structure or size of the Community-scale undertaking or group and in the numbers of employees working in the Member States. If such provisions do not specify that employees (or their representatives) of undertakings or establishments joining the Community-scale undertaking or group after the conclusion of the agreement shall be involved within two years in the replacement or amendment thereof, or shall be represented in the European Works Council or the alternative information and consultation procedure within two years, the central management shall be obliged to set up a new special negotiating body if at least 100 such employees or their representatives so request.
7. The central management shall not be obliged to provide information which would plausibly cause serious harm to or be prejudicial to the functioning of the Community-scale undertaking or group. With respect to the provision of information, the central management may impose a requirement of confidentiality if there are reasonable grounds to do so; a statement shall be issued as early as possible prior to the matter in question being dealt with, indicating the

grounds for imposing the requirement, what written or oral information is covered, for how long it applies and whether there are any persons with regard to whom such confidentiality doesn't need to be maintained.

8. The central management shall ensure that the rights and obligations set out in the agreement are complied with.

Article 12

1. One or more experts may assist the special negotiating body in the negotiations.
2. The expenses reasonably necessary for the special negotiating body to exercise its function shall be borne by the Community-scale undertaking or the controlling undertaking. This shall apply to the cost of consulting one or more experts or of taking legal action only if the Community-scale undertaking or the controlling undertaking has been notified in advance of the expense involved.

Article 13

1. Without prejudice to Article 9(3), each member of the special negotiating body shall have one vote. The special negotiating body's decisions shall be adopted by an absolute majority of the number of votes cast.
2. A decision as referred to in Article 11(2) must be adopted by a two-thirds majority of the number of votes cast.
3. A decision on concluding an agreement as referred to in Article 11(1) must be adopted by at least the number of votes corresponding to a majority of all the votes that can be cast at a plenary meeting of the special negotiating body.

Article 14

The central management shall ensure that the composition of the special negotiating body and the time of any meeting as referred to in Article 11 are made known within the Community-scale undertaking or group.

Paragraph 3

Subsidiary Provisions Governing the Provision of Information and Consultation in the Absence of an Agreement

Article 15

The central management shall be obliged to set up a European Works Council in accordance with this paragraph:

a) if there are indications that the central management will not enter into negotiations with a special negotiating body within six months of the receipt of a request as referred to in Article 8(2);
b) if the central management and the special negotiating body have not concluded an agreement as referred to in Article 11(1) within three years after the receipt of a request as referred to in Article 8(2) or, if the central management has established a special negotiating body of its own accord, within three years of its doing so, unless a decision as referred to in Article 11(2) is in force.

Article 16

1. If the Community-scale undertaking or group has fewer than 5,000 employees, the European Works Council shall consist of one member for each Member State in which the employees work and one, two or three supplementary members respectively for each Member State in which at least one quarter, one half or three-quarters of the employees work.
2. If there are 5,000 or more employees, the European Works Council shall consist of one member for each Member State in which the employees work and one, three, six or nine supplementary members respectively for each Member State in which at least one tenth, one quarter, one half or three-quarters of the employees work.
3. Each member shall be elected or appointed pursuant to the law of the Member State in which he works.
4. The allocation of the seats shall be kept in accordance with subsections 1 and 2; if this leads to a change in the number of supplementary members for a Member State without there having been a new election or appointment to fill such seats, the members holding office for that Member State shall, for the purposes of the relevant provisions concerning the distribution of votes within the European Works Council, together hold as many votes as the number of seats laid down for that Member State under subsections 1 and 2.

Article 17

1. Members of European Works Councils of Dutch establishments and undertakings shall be appointed or elected, or their appointment terminated, in accordance with Article 10, with the proviso that a member's term of office shall last four years.
2. Only employees of the Community-scale undertaking or group may be appointed or elected as members. Membership shall automatically end when a member ceases to be an employee. Persons who are seafarers in the merchant navy shall not be appointed or elected as members.

Article 18

1. The European Works Council shall elect a chairperson and one or more deputy chairpersons from among its members. The chairperson, or if he is not available the deputy chairperson, shall represent the European Works Council in law.
2. The European Works Council may elect from among its members a select committee consisting of three members at most.
3. The European Works Council shall lay down its own rules of procedure. Before these are adopted the central management shall be given the opportunity to state its view. If a select committee is elected, the said rules shall lay down its powers.

Article 19

1. The competence of the European Works Council shall be limited to the provision of information and consultation relating to issues concerning the whole Community-scale undertaking or the whole Community-scale group, or at least two establishments or undertakings of the group in different Member States. This competence shall be confined to matters, which concern all establishments or all undertakings of the group in the Member States or at least two establishments or undertakings of the group in different Member States.
2. The central management and the European Works Council shall meet at least once every calendar year. At such a meeting the European Works Council shall, on the basis of a report drawn up by the central management, be informed about and consulted on the progress of the business of the Community-scale undertaking or group and its prospects. Such information and consultation shall relate in particular to the structure of the Community-scale undertaking or group, its economic and financial situation, the probable development of activities and of production and sales, investments, substantial changes in its organisation, the introduction of new working methods or production processes, environmental care, mergers, relocations, cutbacks or closures of undertakings, establishments or major parts thereof, the employment situation and trends, and collective redundancies.
3. The central management shall inform the European Works Council or the select committee as soon as possible about all particular circumstances or planned decisions affecting the employees' interests to a considerable extent in at least two establishments or undertakings of the Community-scale undertaking or group in different Member States, particularly as regards the relocation or closure of establishments, or collective redundancies.
4. If the European Works Council or the select committee so requests, it shall meet the central management, or another more appropriate level of management within the Community-scale undertaking or group having its own powers of decision on the matters to be dealt with at the meeting, in order to be further informed about and consulted on the circumstances referred to in subsection 3 on the basis of a written report drawn up by the Community-scale

undertaking or group. This meeting shall be held at a time at which such information and consultation is still meaningful. The European Works Council or the select committee may issue an opinion on the report after the meeting or within a reasonable time after the meeting. Those members of the European Works Council who have been co-elected by the employees of the establishments or undertakings directly affected by the measures shall be invited to such a meeting with the select committee. The meeting shall not prejudice the powers of the central management.

5. The central management shall not be obliged to provide information which would plausibly cause serious harm to or be prejudicial to the functioning of the Community-scale undertaking or group. With respect to the provision of information, the central management may impose a requirement of confidentiality if there are reasonable grounds to do so; a statement shall be issued as early as possible prior to the matter in question being dealt with, indicating the grounds for imposing the requirement, what written or oral information is covered, for how long it applies and whether there are any persons with regard to whom such confidentiality doesn't need to be maintained.
6. Before any meeting with the central management, the European Works Council or the select committee shall be entitled to meet without the central management being present. The fourth sentence of subsection 4 shall apply mutatis mutandis.
7. Without prejudice to any obligation on them to maintain confidentiality, the members of the European Works Council shall inform the employees' representatives within the Community-scale undertaking or group or, in the absence of employees' representatives, the workforce as a whole, of the content and outcome of the information and consultation procedure carried out pursuant to this paragraph.
8. The chair of a meeting as referred to in subsection 2 or 4 shall alternate between the central management and the European Works Council, unless otherwise agreed.

Article 20

1. The European Works Council and the select committee may be assisted by experts of their choice insofar as this is necessary for the performance of their duties.
2. The expenses reasonably necessary for the European Works Council and the select committee to exercise their functions shall be borne by the Community-scale undertaking or the controlling undertaking. The obligation to bear the costs of the experts called in by the European Works Council shall be limited to one expert per agenda item, unless the European Works Council and the Community-scale undertaking or the controlling undertaking agree otherwise.
3. The first sentence of subsection 2 shall also apply to the cost of taking legal action, but only on condition that the Community-scale undertaking or the controlling undertaking has been notified in advance of the expense involved.

Article 21

1. At the latest, four years after being established the European Works Council shall decide, in response to a proposal from the central management or otherwise, whether it is desirable to enter into negotiations with the central management on concluding an agreement as referred to in Article 11(1).
2. Articles 11(3) to (6) and 13(1) and (3) shall apply mutatis mutandis, with the proviso that the European Works Council shall replace the special negotiating body.

Article 22

The central management shall ensure that the composition of the European Works Council and the time of any meeting as referred to in Article 19 are made known within the Community-scale undertaking or group.

Chapter 3.
Informing and Consulting Employees in Non-Dutch Community scale Undertakings and Groups of Undertakings

Article 23

If, for the purposes of implementing the Directive in a Member State other than the Netherlands, a special negotiating body or a European Works Council as referred to in the annex to the Directive is set up in a Community-scale undertaking or group, Articles 10 and 17 shall apply mutatis mutandis to Dutch establishments or undertakings in that Community-scale undertaking or group.

Chapter 4.
Final Provisions

Article 24

1. Except for Article 5, this Act shall not apply to a Community-scale undertaking or group which, on the date this Act comes into force, is party to one or more agreements in force which regulate matters concerning the provision of information to and consultation of employees on transnational matters and which have been concluded with an employee's representative body which the Community-scale undertaking or group could deem reasonably representative of the employees in the Member States involved.
2. If such agreements do not specify, or do not specify within five years of this Act coming into force, that employees (or their representatives) of undertakings or establishments joining the Community scale undertaking or group after the conclusion of the said agreements shall be involved within the said period in the replacement or amendment thereof, or shall be represented in the agreed information and consultation procedure, this Act shall apply to the Community-scale undertaking or group after the said period.
3. Article 11(8) shall apply mutatis mutandis.

Article 25

1. For the purposes of Article 9, account need be taken only of those Member States in which the Community-scale undertaking or group has employees and whose legislation implementing the Directive is in force.
2. If an agreement as referred to in Article 11 does not specify that employees (or their representatives) of undertakings or establishments of the Community-scale undertaking or group in Member States, which – in accordance with sub-section 1 – were not taken into account when setting up the special negotiating body, shall be involved in the replacement or amendment of that agreement within two years of such a Member State's legislation implementing the Directive coming into force or shall be represented in the European Works Council or the alternative information and consultation procedure within the said period, that agreement shall be reviewed, taking Article 9 into account.

Article 26

Contains amendments in the Working Hours Act, not related to the information and consultation.

Article 27

This Act shall enter into force on 22 September 1996. If this Act is published in the Staatsblad after 21 September 1996, it shall enter into force on the day following the date of publication of the Staatsblad containing it.

Article 28

This Act shall be cited as the European Works Councils Act.
We order and command that this Act shall be published in the *Staatsblad* and that all ministries, authorities, bodies and officials whom it may concern shall diligently implement it. The Minister of Social Affairs and Employment
A.P.W. Melkert
Published in the Bulletin of Acts and Decrees of 4 February 1997.

b. EWC Act: Amendments of 7 November 2011

ACT OF 7 NOVEMBER 2011

amending of the European Works Councils Act regarding the implementation of Directive 2009/38/EC of the European Parliament and of the Council of 6 May 2009 (OJ 122/2009) recasting Council Directive 94/45/EC on the establishment of a European Works Council or a procedure in Community-scale undertakings and Community-scale groups of undertakings for the purposes of informing and consulting employees

We, Beatrix, by the grace of God Queen of the Netherlands, Princess of Orange-Nassau, etc. etc. etc.

Greetings to all who shall see or hear these presents! Be it known:

Whereas We have considered that, in view of the adoption of Directive 2009/38/EC of the European Parliament and of the Council of 6 May 2009 (OJ 122/2009) recasting Council Directive 94/45/EC, it is necessary to amend a number of provisions of the European Works Councils Act;

We, therefore, having heard the Council of State, and in consultation with the States General, have approved and decreed as we hereby approve and decree:

Article I

The European Works Councils Act shall be amended as follows:

A

Article 1, first subsection, shall be amended as follows:

1. In subsection (a), the words 'Member State' shall be replaced by the words 'involved State'.
2. In subsection (b), the words 'Council Directive 94/45/EC of 22 September 1994' shall be replaced by the words 'Directive 2009/38/EC of the European Parliament and of the Council of 6 May 2009' and the reference to '(OJ L 254)' shall be replaced by '(OJ L 122/2009)'.
3. Subsection (e) shall become subsection (f) and a new subsection (e) shall be inserted which reads as follows:

   '(e) cross-border matters: matters of importance to the entire Community-scale undertaking or the entire Community-scale group of undertakings, or at least two undertakings or establishments of a Community-scale undertaking or Community-scale group of undertakings in two different involved States;'.

4. The full-stop at the end of subsection (f) shall be replaced by a semicolon and the following two subsections shall be added which read as follows:

'(g) provision of information: the transmission of information concerning cross-border issues by the central management or any more appropriate level of management to employees' representatives at such time, in such fashion and with such content as are appropriate to enable employees' representatives to undertake an in-depth assessment of the impact and, where appropriate, to prepare for consultations with the central management or any more appropriate level of management;
(h) consultation: the establishment of dialogue and exchange of views between the central management or any more appropriate level of management and employees' representatives at such time, in such fashion and with such content enabling employees' representatives to express an opinion on the basis of the information provided about proposed measures concerning cross-border issues to which the consultation relates within a reasonable time, which may be taken into account when a decision is taken.'.

B

In Article 1 first subsection (d), second subsection (a) and (b) and third subsection, Article 2, sixth subsection, Article 3 first and second subsections, Article 9 second subsection, Article 16 third subsection, Article 23 and Article 25 second subsection, the words 'Member State' shall in each case be replaced by the words 'involved State'.

C

In Article 1 first subsection (c) and (d), second subsection and third subsection, Article 3 first subsection, Article 6 second subsection, Article 8 second subsection, Article 11 sixth subsection and Article 25 first and second subsections, the words 'Member States' shall in each case be replaced by the words 'involved States'.

D

In Article 2 fifth subsection, the words 'Council Regulation (EEC) No 4064/89 of 21 December 1989' shall be replaced by the words 'Council Regulation (EEC) No 139/2004 of 20 January 2004' and the reference to '(OJ L 395)' shall be replaced by '(OJ L 24/2004)'.

E

In Article 3 second subsection, the words 'Article 4 eighth subsection, Article 7, Article 8 second subsection, Article 11 sixth subsection and Article 19 seventh subsection' shall be replaced by the words 'Article 4 eighth to tenth subsections, Article 7, Article 8 second subsection and Article 11, third subsection (e), sixth subsection and eighth subsection'.

F

Article 4 shall be amended as follows:

1. A sentence shall be added to the third subsection which reads as follows: 'They shall be provided with such facilities which they reasonable need for the performance of their duties'.
2. The eighth and ninth subsections shall be renumbered as the ninth and tenth subsections and a new subsection shall be inserted which reads as follows:

'8. Notwithstanding any of their obligations of confidentiality, employees who are members of a European Works Council or act as representatives under any other procedure for informing and consulting employees shall inform the employee representatives within the Community-scale undertaking or group of undertakings or, if these do not exist, all the employees about the content and results of the information and consultation procedure carried out under this Act.'

3. In the ninth subsection (under the new numbering), the words 'provides an overview of the number of employees working in the Community-scale undertaking or group of undertakings, and the distribution of these employees between the various Member States' shall be replaced by the words 'provide information which is required to open negotiations as referred to in Article 8 first subsection. This information shall in all instances include an overview of the number of employees working in the Community-scale undertaking or group of undertakings, and the distribution of these employees between the various involved States.'

G

In Article 5 second subsection (a) and (b), the words 'Article 19 fifth subsection' shall be replaced by the words 'Article 19 sixth subsection'.

H

Article 7 shall read as follows:

'Article 7

1. A Community-scale undertaking or the controlling undertaking shall provide employees or their representatives with information which is required to open negotiations as referred to in Article 8 first subsection. This information shall in all instances include an overview of the number of employees working in the Community-scale undertaking or group of undertakings, and the distribution of these employees between the various involved States.
2. Where the information as referred to the first subsection changes significantly after the establishment of the special negotiating body, a Community-scale undertaking or the controlling undertaking shall, as quickly as possible after such change, provide an amended overview to the special negotiating body and, where appropriate, to the employees or the representatives of employees

of a Community-scale undertaking or group of undertakings from a involved State who are not yet represented in the special negotiating body.'

I

Article 9 shall be amended as follows:

1. The first subsection shall read as follows:

'1. The number of employee representatives from the Community-scale undertaking or group of undertakings sitting in the special negotiating body shall be such as to ensure that, in respect of each involved State, one member shall be appointed for each portion of employees employed in that State amounting to 10%, or a fraction thereof, of the number of employees working in all the involved States taken together.'

2. The third subsection shall read as follows:

'3. The number of members of the special negotiating body and the allocation of seats shall be in accordance with the provisions of the first subsection. Where the number of members from an involved State changes without any new election or appointment taking place with respect to these seats, the sitting members representing that State shall, for the purposes of Article 13, together have as many votes as correspond to the number of members determined for the involved State in accordance with the first subsection, and shall together represent the employees of the Community-scale undertaking or group of undertakings in the involved State in ratios to be determined by them or, if no agreement can be reached, in proportion to the number of workers whom they represented before such change occurred.'

J

Article 11 shall be amended as follows:

1. In the first subsection, second sentence, the words 'before this meeting takes place' shall be replaced by the words 'before and after this meeting'.
2. The third subsection, subsection (b) shall read as follows:

'(b) the size and composition of the Council, with as balanced a representation of workers as possible, and the period of appointment of its members;'.

3. In the third subsection, subsections (e) and (f) shall become subsections (f) and (g) and a subsection shall be inserted which reads as follows:

   '(e) how the information and consultation of the Council and the information and consultation of employee representatives, as referred to in Article 3 second subsection, are linked together, taking into account their responsibilities;'.

4. The full-stop at the end of subsection (g) (new) at the end of the third subsection shall be replaced by a semicolon and a subsection shall be added which reads as follows:

   '(h) if a select committee is set up within the Council: its composition, appointment procedure, terms of reference and rules of procedure.'

5. In the sixth subsection, the words 'shall contain provisions on the duration of the contract, the manner of negotiating a new agreement' shall be replaced by the words 'shall contain provisions on the date of entry into force, the duration of the agreement, how the agreement may be amended or terminated, where and how to negotiate a new agreement,'.
6. The eighth subsection shall become the ninth subsection and a new eighth subsection shall be inserted which reads as follows:

   '8. If the agreement contains no provisions as mentioned in the third subsection, subsection (e), and decisions are considered which are likely to entail significant changes in work organisation or contractual relations, the information and consultation of the Council and the information and consultation of employee representatives, as referred to in Article 3 second subsection, shall as far as much as possible begin at the same time.'

K

The following shall be added after the word 'experts' in Article 12 first subsection: 'of their choice, including representatives of authorised and recognised employee organisations at Community level, as provided for in Article 154 of the Treaty on the Functioning of the European Union. These experts may, at the request of the special negotiating body, attend the meetings referred to in Article 11 first subsection in an advisory capacity.'

L

Article 14 shall be amended as follows:

1. The number '1.' shall be inserted in front of the existing text.
2. A new subsection shall be added which reads as follows:

   '2. The central management shall also notify the authorised and recognised employee and employers' organisations at Community level, as provided for in Article 154 of the Treaty on the Functioning of the European Union, about the composition of the special negotiating body, and about the start of negotiations as referred to in Article 8 first subsection.'

M

After Article 14, a new Article shall be added to Chapter 2 Section 2 which reads as follows:

'Article 14a

1. If the structure of the Community-scale undertaking or group of undertakings is significantly altered and the relevant agreements contain no relevant provisions, or conflicting provisions, the central administration shall, on its own initiative or at the written request of at least 100 employees or their representatives in at least two companies or establishments in at least two different involved States, start the negotiations referred to in Article 8 first subsection and shall set up a special negotiating body for this purpose.
2. In addition to the members of the special negotiating body elected or appointed in accordance with Article 9, at least three members of the existing European Works Council, or of each of the existing European Works Councils, shall be members of the special negotiating body.
3. During the negotiations as referred to in the first subsection, the existing European Works Council(s) shall function in accordance with the applicable agreement or agreements, or another procedure for informing and consulting workers shall apply if this has been agreed upon.'

N

In Article 15 subsection (b) and Article 21 first subsection, the words 'Article 11 first subsection' shall be replaced by the words 'Article 8 first subsection'.

O

Article 16 shall be amended as follows:

1. The first subsection shall read as follows:

   '1. The number of employee representatives from the Community-scale undertaking or group of undertakings sitting on the European Works Council shall be such as to ensure that, in respect of each involved State, one member shall be appointed for each portion of employees employed in that State amounting to 10 %, or a fraction thereof, of the number of employees working in all the involved States taken together.'

2. The second subsection shall be deleted and the third and fourth subsections shall become the second and third subsections.
3. The third subsection (new) shall read as follows:

   '3. The number of members of the European Works Council and the allocation of seats shall be in keeping with the provisions of the first subsection. Where the number of members from an involved State changes without any new election or appointment taking place with respect to these seats, the sitting members representing that State shall, for the purposes of the relevant provisions concerning the voting weights within the European Works Council, together have as many votes as correspond to the number of members determined for the involved State in accordance with the first subsection, and shall together represent the employees of the Community-scale undertaking or group of undertakings in the involved State in ratios to be determined by them or, if no agreement can be reached, in proportion to the number of workers whom they represented before such change occurred.'

P

Article 18 shall be amended as follows:

1. In the second subsection, the words 'no more than three members' shall be replaced by the words 'no more than five members'.
2. The third sentence in the third subsection shall read as follows: 'If a select committee is elected, the competences of that committee shall be set out in the rules of procedure, which shall also establish the resources necessary to enable it to pursue its activities.'

Q

Article 19 shall read as follows:

'Article 19

1. The information supplied to the European Works Council shall in all events relate to:
   (a) the structure, economic and financial situation, probable development of activities, and production and sales of the Community-scale undertaking or group of undertakings;
   (b) the situation and probable trend of employment, investments, and any substantial changes concerning organisation, introduction of new working methods or production processes, environmental concerns, mergers or downsizing of undertakings, establishments or important parts thereof.
2. The central management shall inform the European Works Council or the select committee as quickly as possible about any exceptional circumstances or decisions which seriously affect the interests of the employees of at least two establishments or undertakings of the Community-scale undertaking or group of undertakings in different involved States, particularly with respect to the relocation or closure of undertakings, establishments or significant parts thereof, or collective redundancies.
3. The consultation of the European Works Council shall be conducted in such a way that the employees' representatives can meet with the central management or any more appropriate level of management within the Community-scale undertaking or group of undertakings with its own decision-making

powers, and can obtain a reasoned response to the opinions they express. Consultation shall in all events relate to the subjects referred to in the first subsection (b) and the second subsection.
4. The central management and the European Works Council shall meet at least once per calendar year. At such meeting, the European Works Council shall be informed and consulted, on the basis of a written report drawn up by the central management, on the progress of the business of the Community-scale undertaking or Community-scale group of undertakings and its prospects. The central management shall ensure that this annual meeting is publicised within the Community-scale undertaking or Community-scale group of undertakings.
5. If the European Works Council or the select committee so requests, it shall meet the central management, or any other more appropriate level of management within the Community-scale undertaking or group of undertakings with its own decision-making powers, so as to be informed and consulted on the basis of a written report drawn up by the Community-scale undertaking or group of undertakings and relating to the circumstances or decisions referred to in the second subsection. The members of the European Works Council who are also elected or appointed by the employees of the establishments or undertakings directly affected by the circumstances or decisions concerned shall also be invited to attend a meeting with the select committee. The meeting shall not affect the powers of the central management.
6. The central management shall not be required to provide information as far as it may reasonably be assumed that this would seriously harm the functioning of the undertakings concerned or would be prejudicial to them. If justifiable reasons exist, the central management may impose confidentiality requirements on the provision of information. It shall, as far as possible, be stated with respect to the specific matter what reasons exist for treating it confidentially, what written or verbal information is covered by the confidentiality requirement, how long it will apply, and whether there are any persons who are not required to maintain such confidentiality.
7. The central management shall give the European Works Council or the select committee the opportunity to meet before and after each meeting with the central management.
8. Unless otherwise agreed, meetings as referred to in the fourth or fifth subsections shall be chaired alternately by the central management and the European Works Council.'

R

Article 24 shall be amended as follows:

1. The first and second subsections shall read as follows:

   '1. This Act shall not apply, with the exception of the provisions of Articles 5 and 14a, to any Community-scale undertaking or group of undertakings which was a party to one or more agreements which entered into force before 5 February 1997, provided that such agreements made provision for information and consultation of employees regarding cross-border issues, and were concluded

with employee representatives whom the Community-scale undertaking or group of undertakings could reasonably consider representative of the employees in the involved States.
2. This Act, as applicable on the day before the entry into force of the Act of 7 November 2011 amending the European Works Councils Act in conjunction with the implementation of Directive 2009/38/EC of the European Parliament and the Council of the European Union of 6 May 2009 (OJL 122/2009) recasting Council Directive 94/45/EC on the establishment of a European Works Council or a procedure in Community-scale undertakings and Community-scale groups of undertakings for the purposes of informing and consulting employees, shall remain applicable with the exception of the provisions of Articles 5 and 14a, to a Community-scale undertaking or group of undertakings which is a party to an agreement as referred to in Article 8, first subsection, relating to the entire workforce, and which was signed or revised in the period from 5 June 2009 to 5 June 2011.'

2. In the third subsection, the words 'eighth subsection' shall be replaced by the words 'ninth subsection'.

S

In Article 25 second subsection, the words 'Article 11' shall be replaced by the words 'Article 8'.

T

Article 26 shall be deleted.

Article II

This Act shall enter into force on 5 June 2011. If the Bulletin of Acts and Decrees (*Staatsblad*) in which this Act is made known is published after 4 June 2011, the Act shall enter into force on the day after its publication in the Bulletin of Acts and Decrees.

We order and command that this Act be published in the Bulletin of Acts and Decrees and that all ministries, authorities, bodies and officials whom it may concern shall diligently implement it.

Done at The Hague, 7 November 2011

Beatrix
The Minister for Social Affairs and Employment,
H.G.J. Kamp
Published on 14 November 2011
The Minister for Security and Justice
I.W. Opstelten

c. EWC Act of 7 November 2011: Consolidated Version[133]

ACT OF 23 JANUARY 1997 for the implementation of Council Directive 94/45/EC of 22 September 1994 on the establishment of a European Works Council or a procedure in Community-scale undertakings and Community-scale groups of undertakings for the purposes of informing and consulting employees (European Works Councils Act)[134]

We Beatrix, by the grace of God Queen of the Netherlands, Princess of Orange-Nassau, etc. etc. etc.

Greetings to all who shall see or hear these presents! Be it known:

Whereas we have considered it necessary to implement Council Directive 94/45/EC of 22 September 1994 on the establishment of a European Works Council or a procedure in Community-scale undertakings and Community-scale groups of undertakings for the purposes of informing and consulting employees;

We, therefore, having heard the Council of State and in consultation with the States-General [Parliament], have approved and decreed as we hereby approve and decree:

Chapter 1.
General Provisions

Article 1

1. In this Act:

   a. 'Involved State' means a Member State of the European Union or another State, which is party to the Agreement on the European Economic Area;
   b. 'Directive' means Directive 2009/38/EC of the European Parliament and of the Council of 6 May 2009 on the establishment of a European Works Council or a procedure in Community-scale undertakings and Community-scale groups of undertakings for the purposes of informing and consulting employees (OJ L 122/2009);
   c. 'Community-scale undertaking' means an undertaking, which for two years has had an average of at least 150 employees in at least two Involved

133. The WEOR was modified over a period of twenty years, as a result of European and/or national changes in legislation (for instance, after the EU Directive became applicable in Great Britain). The most important revision, following the recast, was published in the *Staatsblad* of 14 November 2011 (*see* Ch. 10). All these changes are included in the current WEOR; available at (visited on 1 Oct. 2017): http://wetten.overheid.nl/BWBR0008508/2013-01-01/0/afdrukken+informatie.

134. This English version, compiled by the authors, includes all modifications in the period 1997–2017 to the original text of the WEOR that was published in the Dutch *Staatsblad* (the Bulletin of Acts and Decrees) on 4 Feb. 1997.

States and an average of at least 1,000 employees in the Involved States taken together, unless it belongs to a Community-scale group;

d. 'Community-scale group' means a combination of undertakings consisting of a controlling undertaking as referred to in Article 2 and the undertaking or undertakings over which it exercises control, in which:
   1°. at least two undertakings are situated in different Involved States, and
   2°. for two years at least one undertaking has had an average of at least 150 employees in one Involved State and another undertaking has had an average of at least 150 employees in another Involved State, and
   3°. all the undertakings taken together have for two years had an average of at least 1,000 employees in the Involved States;

e. 'Cross-border matters' means matters of importance to the entire Community-scale undertaking or the entire Community-scale group of undertakings, or at least two undertakings or establishments of a Community-scale undertaking or Community-scale group of undertakings in two different involved States;

f. 'Central management' means, in the case of a Community-scale undertaking, the management of such an undertaking, and in the case of a Community-scale group, the management of the controlling undertaking as referred to in Article 2;

g. 'Provision of information' means the transmission of information concerning cross-border issues by the central management or any more appropriate level of management to employees' representatives at such time, in such fashion and with such content as are appropriate to enable employees' representatives to undertake an in-depth assessment of the impact and, where appropriate, to prepare for consultations with the central management or any more appropriate level of management;

h. 'Consultation' means the establishment of dialogue and exchange of views between the central management or any more appropriate level of management and employees' representatives at such time, in such fashion and with such content enabling employees' representatives to express an opinion on the basis of the information provided about proposed measures concerning cross-border issues to which the consultation relates within a reasonable time, which may be taken into account when a decision is taken.

2. Where the domicile or headquarters of a Community-scale undertaking is not situated in an involved State, the central management shall be deemed to be:
   a a person appointed by the Community-scale undertaking and actually in charge of managing one of its establishments in an involved State, or failing that:
   b the person or persons actually in charge of the establishment employing the greatest number of employees in any one Involved State.

3. Where the domicile or headquarters of the controlling undertaking as referred to in Article 2 is not situated in an Involved State, the controlling undertaking may designate as its representative the management of a group undertaking having its domicile or headquarters in an Involved State. Failing such a designation, the management of the group undertaking which has its domicile or

headquarters in an Involved State and which employs the greatest number of employees in any one Involved State will be deemed to be such.

4. Action or failure to take action by the central management as referred to in article 1, sub 1.e, respectively sub 3 shall be the responsibility of the natural or legal person maintaining the Community-scale undertaking or controlling undertaking or the group undertaking as referred to in article 3.

Article 2

1. In this Act, 'controlling undertaking' means the undertaking within a Community-scale group, which can directly or indirectly exercise a dominant influence over another undertaking and over which no other undertaking exercises a dominant influence directly or indirectly. Unless otherwise shown to be the case, an undertaking shall be presumed to be the controlling undertaking if it:
   a. can appoint more than half of the members of the other undertaking's administrative, management or supervisory body, or
   b. can exercise over half of the voting rights at the general meeting of that other undertaking, or
   c. holds over 50 % of another undertaking's subscribed capital.
2. For the purposes of Article 2, sub 1.a controlling undertaking's rights as regards capital, voting and appointment shall include:
   a. the corresponding rights of other undertakings over which it exercises a dominant influence;
   b. the corresponding rights of any person or body acting in his or its own name but for account of the controlling undertaking or of one or more of its group undertakings.
3. For the purposes of subsection 1, the rights concerning capital and voting shall not be attributed to an undertaking which holds them for account of others.
4. For the purposes of subsection 1, voting rights attached to pledged shares shall be attributed to the creditor if he is authorised to decide how these rights are to be exercised. However, if the shares have been pledged as collateral for a loan, which the creditor has provided in the usual course of his business, the voting rights shall only be attributed to him if he has exercised them on his own behalf.
5. No undertaking as referred to in article 3(5) at (a) or (c) of Council Regulation (EEC) No 139/2004 of 20 January 2004 on the control of concentrations between undertakings[135] (OJ L 24/2004) shall be deemed to be a controlling undertaking.

---

135. *A concentration shall not be deemed to arise where:*

> *a) credit institutions or other financial institutions or insurance companies, the normal activities of which include transactions and dealing in securities for their own account or for the account of others, hold on a temporary basis securities which they have acquired in an undertaking with a view to reselling them, provided that they do not exercise voting rights in respect of those securities with a view to determining the competitive behaviour of that undertaking or provided that they exercise such voting rights only with a view to preparing the sale of all part of that undertaking or of its assets or the sale of those securities and that any such sale takes*

6. The law applicable to an undertaking shall determine whether that undertaking is a controlling undertaking as referred to in subsection 1. If such law is not the law of an Involved State, this matter shall be determined by the law applying to the group undertaking whose management represents the controlling undertaking pursuant to subsection 1(3).
7. If several undertakings within a group meet with one or more of the criteria laid down in subsection 1:
   a. the undertaking which satisfies the criterion laid down in subsection 1, point a shall be deemed to be the controlling undertaking, with the right of appointment regarding the management body taking priority;
   b. where point a. does not lead to an undertaking being deemed to be the controlling undertaking, the criterion laid down in subsection 1, point b shall take priority over that set out in subsection 1, point c;

   without prejudice to proof that another undertaking is able to exercise a dominant influence.

Article 3

1. In this Act the term 'employees' means, insofar as persons working in the Netherlands are concerned, persons working under an employment contract in the Community-scale undertaking or the Community-scale group and, where it applies to persons working in other Involved States, the persons defined as such under the law of the relevant Involved State.
2. For the purposes of Article 4 eighth to tenth subsections, Article 7, Article 8 second subsection and Article 11, third subsection (e), sixth subsection and eighth subsection, 'employees' representatives' means those persons defined as such under the law of the Involved State in which the employees are working; in the case of the Netherlands it means works councils.

Article 4

1. Subsections 2 to 7 shall apply to employees working in the Netherlands who are members of a special negotiating body or of a European Works Council or act as representatives under alternative arrangements for informing and consulting employees.

---

place within one year of the date of acquisition; that period may be extended by the Commission on request where such institutions or companies justify the fact that the sale was not reasonably possible within the period set; (...)

c) the operations (direct or indirect acquisition) carried out by the financial holding companies (...), provided however that the voting rights in respect of the holding are exercised, in particular in relation to the appointment of members of the management and supervisory bodies of the undertakings in which they have holdings, only to maintain the full value of those investments and not to determine directly or indirectly the competitive conduct of those undertakings.

2. Such employees shall retain their entitlement to payment for the period of absence from work necessary to attend a meeting of the special negotiating body or the European Works Council or under the alternative information and consultation arrangements.
3. Insofar as is reasonably necessary for the exercise of their duties they shall be afforded the possibility – during working hours and without loss of pay – of taking part in mutual consultations and deliberations with other persons on matters concerning the performance of their duties, and of undergoing education and training. They shall be provided with such facilities, which they reasonable need for the performance of their duties.
4. They must maintain confidentiality on all business and company secrets which come to their knowledge in their capacity as representatives as well as on all matters designated confidential or whose confidential nature they ought to appreciate in the light of the confidentiality requirement imposed. This also applies to persons who are not employees but perform a function as referred to in subsection 1.
5. The duty of confidentiality shall not apply to anyone brought in for consultation or as an expert as referred to in Articles 12 and 20, provided that the central management or the person who has imposed the confidentiality requirement has given due approval beforehand and the person involved has declared in writing that he undertakes to observe confidentiality on the matter concerned. In such cases the duty of confidentiality shall apply to the person in question.
6. The duty of confidentiality shall not cease upon the termination of a person's function as referred to in subsection 1 or the termination of a person's employment at the undertaking.
7. The employer shall ensure that persons standing, or who have stood, as candidates for a function as referred to in subsection 1, as well as those exercising or having exercised such a function, shall not suffer any disadvantage in their position within the undertaking for that reason.
8. Notwithstanding any of their obligations of confidentiality, employees who are members of a European Works Council or act as representatives under any other procedure for informing and consulting employees shall inform the employee representatives within the Community-scale undertaking or group of undertakings or, if these do not exist, all the employees about the content and results of the information and consultation procedure carried out under this Act.
9. Any employee or employee representative working in the Netherlands may require the employer to provide information which is required to open negotiations as referred to in Article 8 first subsection. This information shall in any case include an overview of the number of employees working in the Community-scale undertaking or group of undertakings, and the distribution of these employees between the various involved States.
10. The employer of an employee who is working in the Netherlands and is appointed or elected as a member of a special negotiating body or of a European Works Council shall report such appointment or election to the central management.

Article 5

1. Any interested person may request the Enterprise Chamber of the Amsterdam Court of Appeal to order implementation of the provisions of this Act, with the exception of Article 4, in so far as the second subsection does not determine otherwise, or of an agreement as referred to in Article 11 or 24. A special negotiating body or the members thereof and a European Works Council established under this Act may not be ordered to pay the costs of such proceedings. Articles 429a to 429t of the Code of Civil Procedure shall apply.
2. The special negotiating body or its members and the European Works Council may request the Enterprise Chamber of the Amsterdam Court to:
   a. remove the prescribed confidentiality, based on article 4, subsections 4 and 5, article 11, subsection 7 or article 19, subsection 6, on the ground that the person who has prescribed the confidentiality, should not have decided to the prescription of confidentiality, in all fairness, in the weighing up of all involved interests;
   b. oblige the person who refused to provide such information, based on article 11, subsection 7, or article 19, subsection 6, to provide this information on the ground that the person should not have decided, in all fairness, in the weighing up of all involved interests, to refuse the information.

Chapter 2.
Informing and Consulting Employees in Dutch Community-Scale Undertakings and Groups

Paragraph 1.
General Provisions

Article 6

1. This chapter shall apply to Community-scale undertakings and controlling undertakings with their domicile or headquarters in the Netherlands.
2. Where the domicile or headquarters of a Community-scale undertaking or controlling undertaking is not situated in an involved State, this chapter shall apply if the domicile or headquarters of the establishment or group undertaking as referred to in Article 1(2) and (3) is situated in the Netherlands.

Article 7

1. A Community-scale undertaking or the controlling undertaking shall provide employees or their representatives with information which is required to open negotiations as referred to in Article 8 first subsection. This information shall in any case include an overview of the number of employees working in the Community-scale undertaking or group of undertakings, and the distribution of these employees between the various involved States.

2. Where the information as referred to the first subsection changes significantly after the establishment of the special negotiating body, a Community-scale undertaking or the controlling undertaking shall, as quickly as possible after such change, provide an revised overview to the special negotiating body and, where appropriate, to the employees or the representatives of employees of a Community-scale undertaking or group of undertakings from an involved State who are not yet represented in the special negotiating body.

Paragraph 2.
Agreements on the Provisions of Information and Consultation

Article 8

1. The central management may set up a special negotiating body for the purpose of entering into negotiations with it concerning an agreement on establishing a European Works Council, whether or not in accordance with paragraph 3, or on making other arrangements for providing information to and consulting employees or their representatives on transnational matters.
2. The central management shall be obliged to set up a special negotiating body as referred to in subsection 1 if a written request to this end has been received from at least 100 employees or their representatives in at least two undertakings or establishments in at least two different involved States. If such a request is received by an establishment or undertaking belonging to a Community-scale undertaking or group, the central management shall ensure that the request is transmitted to it without delay and that the persons who made the request are informed of this.
3. Where the special negotiating body has taken a decision as referred to in Article 11(2), the obligation referred to in subsection 2 above shall not apply during the two years following the taking of such a decision, unless the central management and the special negotiating body have agreed otherwise.

Article 9

1. The number of employee representatives from the Community-scale undertaking or group of undertakings sitting in the special negotiating body shall be such as to ensure that for each involved State one member shall be appointed for each portion of employees employed in that State amounting to 10%, or a fraction thereof, of the total number of employees working in the Community-scale undertaking or group of undertakings in all the involved States taken together.
2. Each member shall be elected or appointed pursuant to the law of the Involved State in which he works.
3. The number of members of the special negotiating body and the allocation of seats shall be in accordance with the provisions of the first subsection. Where

the number of members from a involved State changes without any new election or appointment taking place with respect to these seats, the sitting members representing that State shall, for the purposes of Article 13, together have as many votes as correspond to the number of members determined for the involved State in accordance with the first subsection, and shall together represent the employees of the Community-scale undertaking or group of undertakings in the involved State in ratios to be determined by them or, if no agreement can be reached, in proportion to the number of workers whom they represented before such change occurred.

Article 10

1. With regard to Dutch establishments and undertakings, the members of the special negotiating body shall be appointed, or their appointment terminated, by the works councils set up at such establishments or undertakings.
2. If, in respect of works councils as referred to in subsection 1, one or more central works councils have been established, the said appointment or termination shall be effected by the latter council or councils.
3. If no central works council has been set up, but there are one or more group works councils, the said appointment or termination shall be effected by the latter council or councils.
4. If not all works councils or group works councils are represented in a central works council or group works council, the said appointment or termination shall be effected jointly by the central or group works council or councils and the non-represented works councils.
5. If no works council has been set up, the members of the special negotiating body shall be elected by the entire body of employees working in the Netherlands for the Community-scale undertaking or group. The election shall be by secret written ballot, each employee having one vote. An association of employees having aforementioned employees as its members, with a constitution defining its aim as promoting the interests of its members as employees, active in this manner within the undertaking or group involved and also enjoying full legal capacity, may present a list of candidates for the aforementioned election, provided that it has consulted its members within the undertaking or group on the composition of the list of candidates.
6. For the purposes of subsections 1 to 4, employees of Dutch establishments or undertakings who are not represented in a works council, group works council or central works council will be given the opportunity to express an opinion about the persons to be appointed as members of the special negotiating body.

Article 11

1. After the special negotiating body has been set up, the central management shall convene a meeting with it in order to negotiate an agreement as referred to in Article 8(1). It shall give the negotiating body the opportunity to meet before and after this meeting.
2. As long as no agreement as referred to in Article 8(1) has been concluded, the special negotiating body may decide not to enter into negotiations or to terminate negotiations already in progress.
3. If the central management and the special negotiating body agree to set up a European Works Council, agreement shall also be reached on the Council's rules of procedure. Unless otherwise agreed by the central management and the special negotiating body, the rules of procedure shall at least regulate the following:
   a) the establishments or undertakings of the Community-scale undertaking or group for which the European Works Council is being set up;
   b) the size and composition of the Council, with as balanced a representation of workers as possible, and the period of appointment of its members;
   c) the Council's scope and competence;
   d) the arrangements for informing and consulting the Council;
   e) how the information and consultation of the Council and the information and consultation of employee representatives, as referred to in Article 3 second subsection, are linked together, taking into account their responsibilities;
   f) the frequency, duration and venue of Council meetings;
   g) the financial and material resources to be placed at the Council's disposal;
   h) if a select committee is set up within the Council: its composition, appointment procedure, terms of reference and rules of procedure.
4. If the central management and the special negotiating body agree on a different information and consultation procedure for employees or their representatives not involving the establishment of a European Works Council, the corresponding arrangements shall also be laid down in an agreement. This must include at least the following:
   a) the establishments or undertakings of the Community-scale undertaking or group to which the procedure applies;
   b) the way in which the employees or their representatives are to be informed and consulted on transnational questions which significantly affect employees' interests;
   c) the manner in which employees or their representatives may meet to discuss the questions referred to in point b;
   d) the financial and material resources made available to implement the procedure.
5. The central management and the special negotiating body may agree to set up separate European Works Councils for different parts of the Community-scale undertaking or group, or to apply separate procedures. They may also agree to

set up one or more European Works Councils for one or more parts of the Community-scale undertaking or group and introduce one or more procedures for other parts.

6. The agreement between the central management and the special negotiating body shall contain provisions on the date of entry into force, the duration of the agreement, how the agreement may be amended or terminated, when and how to negotiate a new agreement and for adapting the agreement to changes in the structure or size of the Community-scale undertaking or group and in the numbers of employees working in the Involved States. If such provisions do not specify that employees (or their representatives) of undertakings or establishments joining the Community-scale undertaking or group after the conclusion of the agreement shall be involved within two years in the replacement or amendment thereof, or shall be represented in the European Works Council or the alternative information and consultation procedure within two years, the central management shall be obliged to set up a new special negotiating body if at least 100 such employees or their representatives so request.
7. The central management shall not be obliged to provide information which would plausibly cause serious harm to or be prejudicial to the functioning of the Community-scale undertaking or group. With respect to the provision of information, the central management may impose a requirement of confidentiality if there are reasonable grounds to do so; a statement shall be issued as early as possible prior to the matter in question being dealt with, indicating the grounds for imposing the requirement, what written or oral information is covered, for how long it applies and whether there are any persons with regard to whom such confidentiality doesn't need to be maintained.
8. If the agreement contains no provisions as mentioned in the third subsection (e), and decisions are considered which are likely to entail significant changes in work organisation or contractual relations, the information and consultation of the Council and the information and consultation of employee representatives, as referred to in Article 3 second subsection, shall as far as much as possible, begin at the same time.
9. The central management shall ensure compliance with the rights and obligations set out in the agreement.

Article 12

1. The special negotiating body may be assisted in the negotiations by one or more experts of their choice, including representatives of authorised and recognised employee organisations at Community level, as provided for in Article 154 of the Treaty on the Functioning of the European Union. These experts may, at the request of the special negotiating body, attend the meetings referred to in Article 11 first subsection in an advisory capacity.
2. The expenses reasonably necessary for the special negotiating body to exercise its function shall be borne by the Community-scale undertaking or the controlling undertaking. This shall apply to the cost of consulting one or more

experts or of taking legal action only if the Community-scale undertaking or the controlling undertaking has been notified in advance of the expense involved.

Article 13

1. Without prejudice to Article 9(3), each member of the special negotiating body shall have one vote. The special negotiating body's decisions shall be adopted by an absolute majority of the number of votes cast.
2. A decision as referred to in Article 11(2) must be adopted by a two-thirds majority of the number of votes cast.
3. A decision on concluding an agreement as referred to in Article 11(1) must be adopted by at least the number of votes corresponding to a majority of all the votes that can be cast at a plenary meeting of the special negotiating body.

Article 14

1. The central management shall ensure that the composition of the special negotiating body and the time of any meeting as referred to in Article 11 are made known within the Community-scale undertaking or group.
2. The central management shall also notify the authorised and recognised employee and employers' organisations at Community level, as provided for in Article 154 of the Treaty on the Functioning of the European Union, about the composition of the special negotiating body, and about the start of negotiations as referred to in Article 8, first subsection.

Article 14a

1. If the structure of the Community-scale undertaking or group of undertakings is significantly altered and the relevant agreements contain no relevant provisions, or conflicting provisions, the central administration shall, on its own initiative or at the written request of at least 100 employees or their representatives in at least two companies or establishments in at least two different relevant States, start the negotiations referred to in Article 8 first subsection and shall set up a special negotiating body for this purpose.
2. In addition to the members of the special negotiating body elected or appointed in accordance with Article 9, at least three members of the existing European Works Council, or of each of the existing European Works Councils, shall be members of the special negotiating body.
3. During the negotiations as referred to in the first subsection, the existing European Works Council(s) shall function in accordance with the applicable agreement or agreements, or another procedure for informing and consulting workers shall apply if this has been agreed upon.

Paragraph 3.
Subsidiary Provisions Governing the Provision of Information and Consultation in the Absence of an Agreement

Article 15

The central management shall be obliged to set up a European Works Council in accordance with this paragraph:

a) if there are indications that the central management will not enter into negotiations with a special negotiating body within six months of the receipt of a request as referred to in Article 8(2);
b) if the central management and the special negotiating body have not concluded an agreement as referred to in Article 8(1) within three years after the receipt of a request as referred to in Article 8(2) or, if the central management has established a special negotiating body of its own accord, within three years of its doing so, unless a decision as referred to in Article 11(2) is in force.

Article 16

1. The number of employee representatives from the Community-scale undertaking or group of undertakings sitting on the European Works Council shall be such as to ensure that, in respect of each involved State, one member shall be appointed for each portion of employees employed in that State amounting to 10%, or a fraction thereof, of the number of employees working in all the involved States taken together.
2. Each member shall be elected or appointed pursuant to the law of the Involved State in which he works.
3. The number of members of the European Works Council and the allocation of seats shall be in keeping with the provisions of the first subsection. Where the number of members from an involved State changes without any new election or appointment taking place with respect to these seats, the sitting members representing that State shall, for the purposes of the relevant provisions concerning the voting weights within the European Works Council, together have as many votes as correspond to the number of members determined for the involved State in accordance with the first subsection, and shall together represent the employees of the Community-scale undertaking or group of undertakings in the involved State in ratios to be determined by them or, if no agreement can be reached, in proportion to the number of workers whom they represented before such change occurred.

Article 17

1. Members of European Works Councils of Dutch establishments and undertakings shall be appointed or elected, or their appointment terminated, in accordance with Article 10, with the proviso that a member's term of office shall last four years.
2. Only employees of the Community-scale undertaking or group may be appointed or elected as members. Membership shall automatically end when a member ceases to be an employee.
3. A member of the special negotiating body or of the European Works Councils and his/her deputy, who is seafarer in the merchant navy, has the right to attend the meetings of the special negotiating body or the European Works Council or any other consultation that is organised, if the member or deputy are not offshore or in an harbour in another State than the State of establishment of the shipping company. As far as possible, the meeting will be planned in such a manner that the member or the deputy can easily attend. In case the member or deputy cannot attend the meeting, an effort will be made to receive input of the member or deputy by other means.

Article 18

1. The European Works Council shall elect a chairperson and one or more deputy chairpersons from among its members. The chairperson, or if he is not available the deputy chairperson, shall represent the European Works Council in law.
2. The European Works Council may elect from among its members a select committee consisting of five members at most.
3. The European Works Council shall lay down its own rules of procedure. Before these are adopted the central management shall be given the opportunity to state its view. If a select committee is elected, the competences of that committee shall be set out in the rules of procedure, which shall also establish the resources necessary to enable it to pursue its activities.

Article 19

1. The information supplied to the European Works Council shall in all events relate to:
   a the structure, economic and financial situation, probable development of activities, and production and sales of the Community-scale undertaking or group of undertakings;
   b the situation and probable trend of employment, investments, and any substantial changes concerning organisation, introduction of new working methods or production processes, environmental concerns, mergers or downsizing of undertakings, establishments or important parts thereof.

2. The central management inform the European Works Council or the select committee as quickly as possible about any exceptional circumstances or planned decisions which seriously affect the interests of the employees, particularly with respect to the relocation or closure of undertakings, establishments or significant parts thereof, or collective redundancies.
3. The consultation of the European Works Council shall be conducted in such a way that the employees' representatives can meet with the central management or any more appropriate level of management within the Community-scale undertaking or group of undertakings with its own decision-making powers, and can obtain a reasoned response to the opinions they express. Consultation shall in all events relate to the subjects referred to in the first subsection (b) and the second subsection.
4. The central management and the European Works Council shall meet at least once per calendar year. At such meeting, the European Works Council shall be informed and consulted, on the basis of a written report drawn up by the central management, on the progress of the business of the Community-scale undertaking or Community-scale group of undertakings and its prospects. The central management shall ensure that this annual meeting is publicised within the Community-scale undertaking or Community-scale group of undertakings.
5. If the European Works Council or the select committee so requests, it shall meet the central management, or any other more appropriate level of management within the Community-scale undertaking or group of undertakings with its own decision-making powers, so as to be informed and consulted on the basis of a written report drawn up by the Community-scale undertaking or group of undertakings and relating to the circumstances or decisions referred to in the second subsection. The members of the European Works Council who are also elected or appointed by the employees of the establishments or undertakings directly affected by the circumstances or decisions concerned shall also be invited to attend a meeting with the select committee. The meeting shall not affect the powers of the central management.
6. The central management shall not be required to provide information as far as it may reasonably be assumed that this would seriously harm the functioning of the undertakings concerned or would be prejudicial to them. If justifiable reasons exist, the central management may impose confidentiality requirements on the provision of information. It shall, as far as possible, be stated with respect to the specific matter what reasons exist for treating it confidentially, what written or verbal information is covered by the confidentiality requirement, how long it will apply, and whether there are any persons who are not required to maintain such confidentiality.
7. The central management shall give the European Works Council or the select committee the opportunity to meet before and after each meeting with the central management.
8. Unless otherwise agreed, meetings as referred to in the fourth or fifth subsections shall be chaired alternately by the central management and the European Works Council.

Article 20

1. The European Works Council and the select committee may be assisted by experts of their choice insofar as this is necessary for the performance of their duties.
2. The expenses reasonably necessary for the European Works Council and the select committee to exercise their functions shall be borne by the Community-scale undertaking or the controlling undertaking. The obligation to bear the costs of the experts called in by the European Works Council shall be limited to one expert per agenda item, unless the European Works Council and the Community-scale undertaking or the controlling undertaking agree otherwise.
3. The first sentence of subsection 2 shall also apply to the cost of taking legal action, but only under the condition that the Community-scale undertaking or the controlling undertaking has been notified in advance of the expense involved.

Article 21

1. At the latest, four years after being established the European Works Council shall decide, in response to a proposal from the central management or otherwise, whether it is desirable to enter into negotiations with the central management on concluding an agreement as referred to in Article 8(1).
2. Articles 11(3) to (6) and 13(1) and (3) shall apply *mutatis mutandis*, with the proviso that the European Works Council shall replace the special negotiating body.

Article 22

The central management shall ensure that the composition of the European Works Council and the time of any meeting as referred to in Article 19 are made known within the Community-scale undertaking or group.

Chapter 3.
Informing and Consulting Employees in Non-Dutch Community-scale Undertakings and Groups of Undertakings

Article 23

If, for the purposes of implementing the Directive in an involved State other than the Netherlands, a special negotiating body or a European Works Council as referred to in the annex to the Directive is set up in a Community-scale undertaking or group, Articles 10 and 17 shall apply *mutatis mutandis* to Dutch establishments or undertakings in that Community-scale undertaking or group.

Chapter 4.
Final Provisions

Article 24

1. This Act shall not apply, with the exception of the provisions of Articles 5 and 14a, to any Community-scale undertaking or group of undertakings which was a party to one or more agreements which entered into force before 5 February 1997, provided that such agreements made provision for information and consultation of employees regarding cross-border issues, and were concluded with employee representatives whom the Community-scale undertaking or group of undertakings could reasonably consider representative of the employees in the involved States.
2. This Act, as applicable on the day before the entry into force of the Act of 7 November 2011 amending the European Works Councils Act in conjunction with the implementation of Directive 2009/38/EC of the European Parliament and the Council of the European Union of 6 May 2009 (OJL 122/2009) recasting Council Directive 94/45/EC on the establishment of a European Works Council or a procedure in Community-scale undertakings and Community-scale groups of undertakings for the purposes of informing and consulting employees, shall remain applicable with the exception of the provisions of Articles 5 and 14a, to a Community-scale undertaking or group of undertakings which is a party to an agreement as referred to in Article 8, first subsection, relating to the entire workforce, and which was signed or revised in the period from 5 June 2009 to 5 June 2011.
3. Article 11(9) shall apply *mutatis mutandis*.
4. This article shall apply *mutatis mutandis* to a Community-scale undertaking or group of undertakings, which as of 15 December 1999 would fall under the application of the Act on account solely of the entry into force of the Directive in the United Kingdom, but was at that date already party to one or more agreements, referred to in the first subsection, that have come into effect.

Article 25

1. For the purposes of Article 9, account need be taken only of those involved States in which the Community-scale undertaking or group has employees and whose legislation implementing the Directive is in force.
2. If an agreement as referred to in Article 8 does not specify that employees (or their representatives) of undertakings or establishments of the Community-scale undertaking or group in involved States, which – in accordance with subsection 1 – were not taken into account when setting up the special negotiating body, shall be involved in the replacement or amendment of that agreement within two years of such an involved State's legislation implementing the Directive coming into force or shall be represented in the European Works Council or the alternative information and consultation procedure within the said period, that agreement shall be reviewed, taking Article 9 into account.

(Article 26 – repealed per 15-11-2011)

Article 27

This Act shall enter into force on 22 September 1996. If this Act is published in the *Staatsblad* after 21 September 1996, it shall enter into force on the day following the date of publication of the *Staatsblad* containing it.

Article 28

This Act shall be cited as the European Works Councils Act.

We order and command that this Act shall be published in the *Staatsblad* and that all ministries, authorities, bodies and officials whom it may concern shall diligently implement it.

Signed in The Hague, 23 January 1997

Beatrix
The Minister of Social Affairs and Employment,
A.P.W. Melkert

Part IV. Selected Agreements

a. Introductory remarks, facts and figures
b. Océ – installation agreement 1996
c. Unilever – installation agreement 1996
d. Akzo Nobel – installation agreement 1997
e. TNT – renegotiated agreement 2011
f. Akzo Nobel – renegotiated agreement 2012
g. Unilever – renegotiated agreement 2014

a. *Introductory remarks, facts and figures*

The preparatory work for the implementation of the EWC Directives in the Netherlands and for the drafting of the legal act was embedded in the country's tradition of consultation of social partners and of bipartite and tripartite concertation at national level. In this section, the focus is on the implementation and related developments at company level. This is not meant to be an assessment of the country's record, but serves as an illustration of the practical application of the provisions of the EWC Directives.

EWCs were introduced in the Netherlands in a system of industrial relations with a long tradition of information, consultation and co-determination rights, with works councils at plant, group and central level. Notwithstanding this tradition, employers were rather reluctant to or even against the introduction of new European structures. They stressed that an EWC should not be seen as a natural extension of existing consultation structures. This is in line with the position of the Dutch employers' association VNO that organised a fierce opposition against the drafting and conclusion of the EWC Directive. VNO argued that it was not necessary to create new, additional European structures. During the transposition, the organisation said that too strong consultation rights would lead to an erosion of the national co-decision practices and to serious delays of several months in the decision-making processes.[136] In some companies this position was not only shared by the management, but also by prominent members of the existing councils.[137]

Nevertheless, a series of Dutch undertakings had joined the companies that didn't want to wait for the Directive to dictate them what to do. They preferred voluntary negotiations over mandatory talks. By the time the EWC Directive had to be implemented (22 September 1996), there were 18 voluntary ('Article 13') agreements of Dutch origin signed in multinational companies.[138] The agreements at Océ (section b) and Unilever (section c) included here stem from that period and refer explicitly to article 13 of the EWC Directive.

The most updated data show that since then the amount of concluded Dutch origin agreements has increased to an overall total of 65 agreements (next to 29 agreements that in the meantime are no longer effective).[139] In the years after the Directive was implemented, a series of agreements was concluded in a relatively representative part of the larger Dutch transnational companies, based on the Directive. The initial agreement at Akzo Nobel (section d) was concluded in that period.

The modification of the 1994 Directive, leading to the EWC Recast Directive (treated in Chapter 7) did not bring a new dynamic. However, the text of the EWC

136. VNO letter to the Dutch parliament, 19 April 1996, quoted in a report of the parliament's deliberations, May 1996. https://zoek.officielebekendmakingen.nl/dossier/24641/kst-24641-5?resultIndex=33&sorttype=1&sortorder=4.

137. One of the authors was engaged as expert in the negotiations of some 50 EWC agreements all over Europe.

138. Paul Marginson, Mark Gilman, Otto Jacobi and Hubert Krieger, 'Negotiating European Works Councils: an analysis of agreements under Article 13', Interim Report, European Foundation for the Improvement of Living and Working Conditions, 1998. https://www.eurofound.europa.eu/sites/default/files/ef_files/pubdocs/1998/39/en/1/ef9839en.pdf.

139. According to the EWC portal http://www.ewcdb.eu/ (visited 14 Dec. 2017).

Recast Directive was one of the references for renegotiations. Here included are four renegotiated agreements, spread over the last 8 years, TNT (section e), Akzo Nobel (section f), Unilever (section g) and Heineken (section h). The TNT-agreement refers explicitly to the EWC Recast Directive. The other three agreements fit in a group of companies that has reassessed the functioning of the EWC on a regular basis. These companies have, in the meantime, decided to continue with an update based on, for instance, a 4-year rhythm or have opted for a more permanent agreement.

In practice, the operational experiences are quite mixed. The aim here is not to assess and compare these experiences in detail. But, it can be said that, for instance, the possibility for European Works Councils to appeal to the Enterprise Chamber of the Amsterdam Court is a strong instrument. The Netherlands has always been classified as being part of a group of countries with established structures for employee information and consultation within enterprises at national and plant level, guaranteed by law or by negotiated agreements. An early comparative study, published in 1998, qualifies the Netherlands, in terms of operational success stories, as a particularly rich source of examples. The study categorises the Netherlands in the group of countries with 'a relatively tight fit between existing representation and/or information and consultation arrangements and EWCs'.[140]

In several areas, it is possible to identify the influence of the already existing 'tradition' of consultation practices. EWC's, therefore, can play a role in consultations on transnational issues and, regularly, are asked for advice. For instance, at Unilever, the EWC has, according to a case study published in 2007, developed rapidly from the late 1990s onwards. The EWC of the group was consulted and could intervene in two cases of transnational restructuring. One was related to the closure of a Danish subsidiary, where local employees were consulted as a result of EWC-initiatives and an advice on a social plan was taken over by the management. In a similar Dutch/Belgium case Unilever agreed to look for alternative employment for the involved employees as suggested by the EWC. The Unilever EWC thus changed from a purely information forum to a proactive and strategic instrument of European employee interest representation and a platform of consultation and negotiation on transnational issues with representatives of the European Unilever management. The 2007 case study calls the EWC 'the most important instrument and channel for the articulation of employee demands throughout Europe in nearly all crucial issues and cases. In 2006, for example, the EWC was the main dialogue/negotiation partner for the European management on issues like the restructuring/relocation of the Unilever Shared Services Centre, the future of the Unilever frozen food division and a reorganisation plan for supply chains'.[141]

140. Several Dutch experiences are listed in one of the first impact assessments, as published by Eurofound. *See*: *The impact of European Works Councils*, Eurofound, Observatory: EurWORK, 1998. https://www.eurofound.europa.eu/printpdf/observatories/eurwork/comparative-information/the-impact-of-european-works-councils.

141. At https://www.eurofound.europa.eu/sites/default/files/ef_publication/field_ef_document/ef0665enc5.pdf.

b. Océ – installation agreement 1996

Océ-van der Grinten – European Information and Consultation Forum / September 1996

PREAMBLE

The on-going integration of the common European market more and more requires provisions regarding information and consultation of the employees belonging to the same European organisation. Such provisions should be complementary to the practices and procedures for employee representation as already existent in the various operating companies (OPCO's).

The Board of Executive Directors of Océ-van der Grinten NV (the Board), the parent company of the Océ Group, desires to establish a European Information and Consultation Forum (the EF) for the employees of the OPCO's within the European Union, so as to channel the relevant information and create structured communication, practices and procedures between the Head Office and the said employees.

EF shall confer in a cooperative spirit with due regard to mutual rights and obligations of the participants, and promote a fruitful dialogue between the Board and the Employees of the Océ Group.

To fulfil these objectives the representatives of employees of the eligible OPCO's in the European Union and the Board of Océ-van der Grinten N.V. agreed upon the following rules.

This Agreement is an Agreement as referred to in Article 13 of the EU Directive 94/45/EC of 22 September 1994.

Rules

Article 1: Apportionment

Océ-van der Grinten N.V. and each OPCO within the European Union of which the voting rights are held for more than 50% directly or indirectly by Océ-van der Grinten N.V. are invited to participate in the EF.

A participating OPCO employing over 150 people has the right to delegate one representative; participating OPCO's employing over 1000 people are entitled to delegate a second representative.

Article 2: Chair

The EF is chaired by the Chairman of the Board. When he is unable to attend a meeting the chair is taken by another member of the Board.

Article 3: Membership

Election of the EF representatives should aim at a fair representation of the employees in the pertaining OPCO. The parties hereto acknowledge that a certain degree of continuity in the group of EF representatives is necessary in order to function in the most efficient and effective way. Eligible as EF representatives are employees who have a service with the participating OPCO at the date of the pertaining EF meeting.

Since the delegates are representatives of the personnel, Chief Executive Officers (CEO's), members of the management teams and Human Resources Officers are not eligible.

Article 4: Organisational Matters

The EF shall install a Committee which shall consist of 3 EF representatives and 2 members among whom the EF secretary on behalf of the Board. The Committee shall appoint its own chairman and shall decide in all matters by normal majority of votes.

The Committee shall draw up the agenda for the EF meetings. All representatives may suggest subjects for the agenda up to one month prior to the EF meetings.

The Committee shall also be entrusted with the organisational matters concerning the EF meetings.

The Board will appoint the EF secretary.

The EF secretary shall be entrusted with the assistance and support by facilities provided by the Board. The EF secretary shall in agreement with the Committee draw up a report of each meeting and shall circulate this to the EF representatives.

Article 5: Representation

The CEO of a participating OPCO, which is entitled to delegate one or two representatives, is responsible for the proper organisation of their election or nomination.

Deputy representatives will be appointed according to the same procedures in order to substitute for the full members when the latter would be unable to attend a meeting.

All local election procedures for election or nomination should comply with national legislation procedures and good practices.

Article 6: Languages and Translation

As English is the common language used in the Océ Group, the communication language in the EF meetings will be English. Where deemed necessary, facilities to learn English will be made available to the EF representatives. On the basis of the level of knowledge of English within the group of EF representatives, the Committee may decide on a case by case basis which translation facilities are required for each EF meeting, taking into account that best efforts will be used to minimise the number of languages used at such meetings.

Article 7: Information and Consultation

The issues the EF will deal with refer to business, financial and employment matters of the Océ Group which have impact on at least two of the participating OPCO's.

On a regular basis the representatives are informed and consulted on important developments in the Océ Group. To this end, the Chairman of EF will send to them the Annual and Quarterly Financial Reports, and Press Releases published by Océ.

Other important information may refer in particular to the actual situation and projected developments of:

- The organisational structure of the Océ Group

- The state of the business
- The financial results
- Strategic mainlines and future product assortment
- Major investments and disinvestments
- Employment trends and head-count figures
- Important changes in working methods regarding product development, manufacturing and logistics, information systems, sales and field service operations
- Mergers and take-overs.

The consultation means the exchange of views and establishment of a dialogue between EF representatives and the Board.

All information given to the EF is also made available to the CEO's of each OPCO within the European Union.

Article 8: Subsidiarity

Matters which are already subject to information or consultation bodies at OPCO level, are not dealt with by EF. In case such issue will have impact on at least two of the participating OPCO's from two different countries in the European Union, the EF representatives from these countries may suggest such issue to the Committee. The Committee will decide in close consultation with the Chairman whether such issue will be put on the agenda.

The authority of local works councils is not to be affected and the decision making by the OPCO Management is not to be hampered.

Article 9: Meetings

The EF meets at least once a year. This regular meeting is within one month after the publication of the annual report of the Océ Group. The meetings shall take place in Venlo, and are convened by the EF Secretary.

The agenda and all materials and documents relevant thereto, will be sent by the EF Secretary to all Employees representatives not later than two weeks prior to each meeting; barring unforeseen circumstances.

In case of extraordinary circumstances which have significant impact on the interest of employees in several countries within the European Union, the Committee shall be informed. In such cases the Committee may involve the EF representatives from the countries concerned and may recommend to the Chairman to call an extraordinary EF meeting.

The EF representatives will have the possibility to hold a preparatory meeting prior to the EF meeting.

Article 10: Experts

Should expert advice be deemed necessary by the Committee or the majority of the EF representatives in connection with one or more specific items on the agenda of the EF, the Committee may retain an expert for such item.

Océ's internal expertise should be used as much as possible.

If useful for the discussion about such an item in an EF meeting, the expert may be invited by the Committee to attend the relevant part of the EF meeting.

Article 11: Protection

Océ-van der Grinten N.V. shall ensure that EF representatives shall enjoy the same protection against negative consequences in exercising their EF functions as provided by the legal provisions in force in their country of employment.

Article 12: Facilities and Means

The required facilities such as meeting rooms will be made available by the Board. The representatives will receive the required means to adequately perform their duty.

Time consumption and travel and lodging expenses are fixed in concert with the CEO of the OPCO by which the representative is delegated.

Article 13: Communication Between EF Representatives and Local Employees

EF representatives are expected to pass the information received to the other employees of their OPCO according to a procedure agreed with their CEO.

Article 14: Confidentiality

EF representatives are not authorized to reveal any information which has expressly been provided to them in confidence. This obligation shall continue to apply, even after the expiry of their office of representation.

In specific cases and under the conditions laid down by national legislation, the management is not obliged to transmit information when its nature is such, that transfer of such information would seriously harm the functioning of the Océ-Group, Océ-van der Grinten N.V. or its subsidiaries or would be prejudicial to them.

Article 15: Transitional Arrangements

The EF will function initially on a transitional basis for a period of three years following the first meeting, (as from July 4, 1996).

At the end of the transitional period, conditions for composition and running of the EF will be renewed, taking into consideration in particular the development and the level of the Group activities in Europe.

Article 16: Applicable Laws

Dutch law is applicable to these Rules.

Executed and undersigned by the Board and the EF Representatives as follows:
Océ-van der Grinten N.V.

Venlo, September 4, 1996

The EF Representative(s) of OPCO … … … … … … …

Date: Name: Signature:

c. Unilever – installation agreement 1996

Unilever – Unilever European Works Council (UEWC) / September 1996

PREAMBLE

- The internationalization of business and the changes in Europe, also in terms of the European Internal Market, are bringing about a transformation in the way employees think and in company structures. In this integration process, which is important for both sides, economic and social aspects form the basis for a future-orientated company policy.
- In order to create a framework for effective exchange of information and consultation at a European level, Unilever's management and employee representatives have agreed upon the establishment of a Unilever European Works Council.
- The parties accept that Unilever is in many respects a unique organisation, comprising a multitude of businesses in several industries and based upon local decentralised profit responsibility. The objective of this agreement therefore is to devise a European Works Council which fosters this organisation and positively supports the best exchange of information and consultation in the existing consultative bodies in the companies.
- In this context, a significant role is played by fair cooperation based on mutual trust between the management, employees and their representatives. This involves comprehensive and timely mutual exchange of information, as well as the opportunity for all those involved to introduce their ideas into the dialogue. A supranational exchange of information and views will promote mutual understanding and willingness to cooperate.
- In so far as procedures and definitions are not laid down in this agreement or in the Annexes hereto, these will be settled on a case-by-case basis in the spirit of collaboration based on mutual trust, and taking account of the rights and duties of both contracting partners.

1. Aim and Status of the Agreement

The following Agreement under the terms of Article 13 of the EU Directive (94/45/EC) dated 22nd September 1994 governs supranational information and consultation of employees and their representatives.

2. Scope

This Agreement shall apply to all Unilever companies in the European Economic Area, including in the United Kingdom and in Switzerland. Companies joining and leaving Unilever NV/PLC in the European Economic Area will be automatically included in the Agreement or respectively excluded from the same. The fact that companies join or leave Unilever PLC/NV shall have no influence on validity of this agreement.

3. Composition

The UEWC is composed of a management delegation with authority and of an employee delegation.

Exclusively employees of a Unilever company in the scope of the UEWC shall enter into consideration as members of the employees' delegation.

The number of employee representatives who may be seconded to the UEWC from a country is based on the total number of those employed in the respective country.

In this regard, the following key shall apply:

Number of Unilever employees in the country	*Number of UEWC employee representatives to be seconded*
< 2,000	1
2,000–7,000	2
7,001–20,000	3
> 20,000	4

Selection or appointment of employee representatives

The employee representatives shall be elected or appointed in accordance with the national legislation, collective labour agreements or with current practice.

The employee representatives thus elected or appointed are considered to be fully representative of all Unilever employees in their country including employees who join the Unilever NV/PLC during his/her full term of office.

The term of office of each employee representative in the UEWC shall correspond to his/her national practice, but shall not be longer than 4 years.

If necessary, on business or on personal grounds, the succession of an employee representative should be organised in line with the agreed procedure on the selection of employee representatives.

Re-election or re-appointment shall be possible.

The employee members of the UEWC will enjoy the protection that the national legislation and/or practice in their country of employment provides for. By virtue of exercise of their mandate, they may neither receive preferential treatment, nor may they be disadvantaged; they must receive leave of absence for attending the meetings referred to in this Agreement, in accordance with national praxis.

4. Organization

a) The management shall appoint an authorized Management Representative.
b) The employee delegation will elect from amongst its members and for its organisation a Chairman and a Secretary.
c) Furthermore the employee delegation in the UEWC may establish a Coordination Committee, which shall consist of the Chairman and the Secretary of the employee delegation and of up to 4 further employee representatives. The tasks

of this Coordination Committee shall be laid down by the employee delegation in rules and procedures. These rules and procedures shall be submitted to the management for notification.

This coordination committee shall meet twice per year.

d) Once a year a plenary UEWC meeting shall take place in Rotterdam under the chairmanship of the management.

e) The employee delegation may hold a preparatory session on the day before the plenary meeting. After the plenary meeting, the employee delegation may organise a debriefing meeting. In total, the preliminary session, plenary meeting and debriefing meeting should not take up more than two days, excluding travelling time.

f) The employee delegation shall be entitled, in the preliminary session and debriefing meeting, as well as in the meetings of the Coordination Committee (art. 4c), to invite internal or external experts of their choice in conjunction with topics which will be dealt with in the UEWC. in so far as this incurs costs which the employee delegation wishes the management to bear, prior consent shall be required.

g) It is agreed that all participants shall endeavour to reduce the number of languages used. For this purpose, the employee representatives shall be offered an English course at the expense of their employing company.

If necessary and if feasible, interpretation facilities shall be offered during the meetings. The extent of these facilities shall be jointly determined in the UEWC.

All written information prepared by the management, as well as the agenda, Minutes and the Joint Statement, shall only be drawn up in English. English shall be the authoritative language.

Translation of all written information, into the respective mother tongue may be undertaken in the respective home country at the expenses of the company concerned.

h) The costs connected to the meetings, as well as travelling, accommodation and board for the participants, shall be borne by the company. With regard to travelling undertaken by the employee representatives, the travel policy of the respective Unilever companies shall apply.

5. Competence

a) The subjects of information and consultation shall in particular be the matters listed below, being of a cross-border nature, and which affect at least two countries within the geographical scope of application of this Agreement:
- Economic and financial situation
- Progress of the business in the different sectors
- Probable trends in employment
- Investments
- Significant organizational and structural changes
- Introduction of new working methods and production procedures
- Relocation of production and relocation of product lines

- Workforce reduction in or closure of operational units or major parts thereof, as well as collective redundancies.

  By way of example, further themes may be:
- Safety of employees and Environmental protection
- Training
- The situation of women

b) The UEWC shall not infringe the authority and competence of the respective national or local management and the respective national or local employees' representative bodies. Matters relating to employees and companies in just one country shall remain under the exclusive competence of the interlocutors in such country under the rules usual thereto (e.g. matters in conjunction with state legislation or national collective labour agreements; salaries, wages, working conditions, negotiations of any kind; personal or political matters).

c) Tasks of the Chairman and the Secretary of the employee delegation and of the appointed management representative (art. 4a) on behalf of the UEWC chairman:
   - Preparation of the agenda for the annual plenary meeting
   - The keeping of Minutes at the annual plenary meeting
   - Drafting of the Joint Statement of the annual plenary meeting for use in communication to all employees to whom this Agreement shall apply. Local rules shall apply to this communication.
   - Point of contact between meetings, for example in the event of special circumstances significantly affecting employees' interests in several countries. They consult amongst themselves on the necessity and format of all further information and consultation. This could imply the involvement of the Coordination Committee or the respective employee representatives in the UEWC of the countries concerned.

6. Confidentiality

The employee delegation must maintain confidentiality (i.e. based on their national legislation or practices) on all business and company secrets which they learn in their capacity as representatives as well as on all matters designated confidential or whose confidential nature they ought to appreciate in the light of the confidentiality requirement being imposed. This also applies to third party experts.

The duty of confidentiality shall not be terminated by cessation of their representative mandate or by cessation of the involved person's employment at the undertaking.

Management shall not be obliged to provide information which would be prejudicial to the business interests of Unilever.

7. Duration

This Agreement shall come into force on the day upon which it is signed and shall apply until 31.01.2001. An evaluation of its workings shall be started in September 1999, leading – if necessary – to a renegotiation of the agreement that should then take effect on 1 February 2001. If by that time, no agreement is reached, the 'Subsidiary Provisions governing information and consultation in the absence of an agreement' in the Dutch EWC transposition law will apply.

In so far as differences of opinion shall arise between the management and the employee representatives as to the content and interpretation of this Agreement, these should be settled within the framework of voluntary negotiations.

Dutch law shall apply.

Rotterdam. 20 September 1996

(Signed by European and national management and employee representatives).

Annex 1

Definitions

Information:
The provision of data and the explanations of such data, orally or in writing.

Consultation:
Exchange of views and establishment of a dialogue. Consultation will take place in the course of the normal decision taking process, where possible, prior to the implementation of the decision and will concern the principles underlying the decision.

Employee:
All regular staff considered as 'employees' according to the legislation/practice in each Member State of employment.

Unilever company:
Any company of which Unilever NV/PLC or companies belonging to the Concern hold the majority (i.e. 51%) of the equity.

European Economic Area:
The EEA contains the countries as described in the geographical scope of that Treaty.

Management:
Management in this agreement refers to the management representatives responsible for the execution of this agreement on behalf of the Central Management.

Employee delegation:
The employee delegation is the group of employee representatives in the UEWC as a whole.

Employee representatives:
An employee representative is an employee of a Unilever company elected or appointed as described under Article 3.

Annex 2

Country	*UEWC*
Austria	2
Belgium	2

Country	*UEWC*
Denmark	1
Finland	1
France	3
Germany	4
Greece	1
Ireland	1
Italy	3
Netherlands	3
Portugal	1
Spain	2
Sweden	2
Switzerland	1
UK	4
Total	31

Number of UEWC Employee Representatives per country as per August 1996.

d. Akzo Nobel – installation agreement 1997

AkzoNobel Group / February 1997 / AGREEMENT ON THE EUROPEAN FORUM IN AKZO NOBEL

between the signatories

1. Employees representatives of the of the Akzo Nobel Group (as defined below) in the countries of the territory (as defined below),
   and
2. Akzo Nobel N.V., an undertaking whose registered office is in Arnhem in the Netherlands

PREAMBLE

The contracting parties intend to enter into a dialogue on social issues within the AkzoNobel Group with a view to making an active contribution to effective collaboration and cooperation within the group.

For that purpose the contracting parties intend to create a transnational platform with a view to providing the opportunity for Akzo Nobel N.V. and its European employees to meet in a spirit of cooperation and to open two-way communication on questions of transnational interest and transnational significance.

For these reasons the following is hereby agreed:

INTRODUCTION – DEFINITIONS

1. The 'Akzo Nobel Group' comprises all legal persons and partnerships within the territory, which are controlled either directly or indirectly by Akzo Nobel N.V., i.e. where Akzo Nobel N.V. holds the majority of the shares or votes.
2. 'Consultation' means an exchange of views and an entering into a dialogue between the delegates and the management.
3. 'Coordinating Committee' refers to the Forum Committee described in Point 2.7.
4. 'Delegates' are the members of the Forum appointed in accordance with § 2.
5. 'Directive' means EU Directive 95/45/EC of 22 September 1994 on procedures for informing and consulting employees on a transnational basis.
6. 'Forum' refers to the Akzo Nobel European Forum to be set up in accordance with the present agreement.
7. 'Forum Meetings' are the meetings of the delegates.
8. 'Joint Meeting' are meetings at which both the Forum members and the management take part.
9. 'Management' refers to the person(s) appointed and duly authorised by Akzo Nobel N.V. to represent the Akzo Nobel Group in all contacts with the Forum. The Forum shall be informed about the appointments in good time.
10. 'National Coordinator' refers to the manager appointed by Akzo Nobel N.V. in a given country who acts as the contact person between the employees in the country concerned and Akzo Nobel N.V. with a view to due implementation of the present agreement.

11. The 'territory' comprises the Member States of the European Union plus Norway.

§1 – THE AKZO NOBEL EUROPEAN FORUM

1.1 The contracting parties hereby establish the Forum for the purpose of informing and consulting the employees of Akzo Nobel Group on a transnational basis on issues concerning the Akzo Nobel Group as a whole or at least two establishments or companies of the Akzo Nobel Group in different countries of the territory as described in detail in § 3.

1.2 The present agreement lays down rules for cooperation between Akzo Nobel N.V., represented by the management, and the delegates who constitute the Forum.

1.3 The rights and obligations pursuant to national laws and provisions and to other decisions on employee participation shall not be effected by the present agreement. This means that the rights and obligations relating to employee participation which apply to the various companies of the Akzo Nobel group pursuant to national legislation shall remain in effect without restriction.

1.4 The rules of procedure shall be elaborated by the Coordinating Committee in accordance with the provisions of the present agreement and shall be approved after discussion with the management at a Forum meeting.

§2 – CONSTITUTION OF EWC AN AND SELECT COMMITTEE

2.1 The Forum shall be composed of one member for each country of the territory in which there are undertakings of the Akzo Nobel Group with employees. These members shall be supplemented by one, two, three, five, seven or nine additional members for each country in which at least one twentieth, one tenth, one sixth, one quarter, half or three-quarters of all the employees concerned are employed.

2.2 The Forum delegates shall be elected in accordance with the laws and/or practice of the respective countries which they represent. The local circumstances shall thereby be taken into account, and efforts shall be made to seek appropriate representation of the employees of the undertakings of the Akzo Nobel Group in the country concerned. The national coordinators shall be required to ensure that these elections are conducted properly in their respective countries.

2.3 The names of the delegates thus elected shall be communicated to the Forum secretariat in writing by the national coordinators.

2.4 The contracting parties are aware of the fact that it is necessary to have a certain degree of continuity in the group of delegates for the Forum to be able to perform its duties efficiently and effectively. It is therefore agreed that the term of office of the members of the Forum shall be 4 years unless it is terminated in accordance with the provision of the present agreement or national rules and/or practice. In appointing the management representatives Akzo Nobel N.V. shall ensure that continuity is also guaranteed on the part of the management.

2.5 Only persons who are employed in one of the undertakings of the Akzo Nobel Group within the territory shall be eligible as Forum delegates.

2.6 Where the total number of employees of the undertakings of the Akzo Nobel Group changes in one or several countries of the territory with consequences for the representation of the employees in the country or countries concerned and/or for the distribution of places in the Forum, appropriate measures shall be taken to adapt the composition of the Forum accordingly within one year. The following interim arrangements shall apply in this case:

a) In the event of an increase in the number of employees as the result of acquisition(s), the additional employees shall be represented by the delegates in the country or countries concerned.

b) In the event of a decrease in the number of employees as the result of the sale of an undertaking or undertakings or other such transactions with the result that the representation right of the delegates concerned lapses, substitute members shall be elected as soon as possible.

Where it proves necessary to elect new delegates, the national coordinator(s) shall ensure that the procedures are conducted properly in accordance with the national provisions and/or practice.

2.7 The delegates will shall elect a Coordinating Committee composed of the chairperson of the Forum and two delegates. The Coordinating Committee shall have the task of supporting communication between the management and the Forum. (Cf. Point 6 for the relevant details.)

§3 – SUBJECT OF INFORMATION AND CONSULTATION

3.1 The Forum shall be informed and consulted on the development of the activities of the Akzo Nobel Group within the territory and on the future prospects in accordance with the provisions laid down in Point 1.1.

3.2 The information and consultation referred to in Point 3.1 shall relate in particular to the following subjects concerning the Akzo Nobel Group:

– the structure of the undertaking
– its economic and financial position
– its probable development of business, production and sales
– the situation and probable trend of employment
– investment and divestments
– substantial changes concerning organization
– the introduction of new working methods or production processes
– the restructuring of production
– mergers
– cut-backs or closures of undertakings, establishments or important parts thereof
– collective redundancies

– subjects selected by the management and the Coordinating Committee from time to time in view of their significance.

3.3 Where there are exceptional circumstances affecting employees' interests in at least two countries of the territory to a considerable extent, the Coordinating Committee shall be informed.

§4 – ORDINARY MEETINGS

4.1 An ordinary meeting (called the 'annual conference') shall be held every year at the invitation of the management within two months of the publication of the annual report of Akzo Nobel N.V..

4.2 The annual meeting shall comprises three consecutive individual sessions:
- a Forum meeting to prepare for the joint meeting
- a joint meeting
- a Forum meeting to evaluate the results of the joint meeting.

The annual conference shall be held on two consecutive days.

4.3 The management and the chairperson of the Forum shall share the joint meetings alternately unless other arrangements are agreed between the Coordinating Committee and the management. The management may, on request, take part in the meetings accompanied by expert employees from the Akzo Nobel Group.

4.4 At the Joint Meeting the Forum shall be informed and consulted by the management on the basis of its report on the development of the activities of the Akzo Nobel Group within the territory and the future prospects, in accordance with Point 3.1 and 3.2. In the course of the joint meeting the management shall answer all questions relating to the subjects enumerated in Point 3.2 subject to the restrictions pursuant to Point 7.4.

§5 – EXTRAORDINARY CIRCUMSTANCES AND MEETINGS

Where extraordinary circumstances occur as defined in Point 3.3, the Coordinating Committee shall be entitled also to include the delegates from the countries concerned who are not members of the Coordinating Committee insofar as it has good reasons to consider this necessary. In such cases an extraordinary session can also be convened in agreement between the management and the Coordinating Committee; the management and the Coordinating Committee shall decide on the agenda and participants for such a session. The extraordinary meeting shall also comprise the meetings mentioned in Point 4.2. The provisions of § 4 shall also apply here accordingly, where relevant.

§6 – ORGANISATIONAL ARRANGEMENTS

6.1 The Forum shall be supported by a secretariat, which shall be provided by Akzo Nobel N.V.. The Secretariat shall attend to the organisation of all of the

Forum meetings in accordance with the instructions to be agreed on by the management and the Coordinating Committee.

6.2 Apart from the meetings held pursuant to § 5, the Coordinating Committee shall convene twice a year. One of these meetings shall serve to prepare for the annual conference and shall be held at least 6 weeks before that conference. The coordinating Committee shall decide on the agenda of the second meeting.

6.3 The agenda for the joint meeting shall be determined jointly by the Coordinating Committee and the management. The agenda for the joint session, the report mentioned in Point 4.4, and all other documents shall be sent out by the secretariat to all participants and national coordinators at least four weeks in advance.

6.4 The secretariat shall be responsible for drawing up the minutes of the joint meetings. The minutes shall be presented to the Coordinating Committee and the management for approval, after which they shall be sent to the delegates and national coordinators.

A summary report of the joint meeting shall be agreed on by the Coordinating Committee and the management during the meeting. That report shall be sent to the delegates and national coordinators for translation and distribution to the employees in the countries concerned in accordance with national legislation and practice.

6.5 The Coordinating Committee shall attend to forwarding any information received in the intervening period to the other delegates.

6.6 All contributions in writing and documents shall be drawn up in English. The working language ate the meetings shall be in English, but interpreting and translation facilities shall be provided for the delegates depending on their languages needs.

6.7 All participants at the meetings shall endeavour to restrict the number of languages used at the meetings to a minimum. Where necessary, the delegates shall be given opportunities through their national coordinators to learn English.

6.8 The national coordinators shall, in agreement with the delegate(s) in their respective countries, ensure that that (those) delegate(s) and the employees he/she/they represent(s) are adequately consulted before the annual conference and before any extraordinary meetings and also that there is adequate reporting after the meetings. For that purpose the national coordinators shall have the documents which are distributed to the employees in their respective countries translated where necessary.

§7 – CONFIDENTIALITY

7.1 The Forum delegates shall not be entitled to disclose any confidential information.

7.2 Before any confidential information is communicated to the Forum, the Coordinating Committee or the delegates, the management may from time to time call on the delegates concerned to confirm that that information will not be communicated to third persons (with the exception of the other delegates) up to a certain point in time. However, a request of this nature shall require prior discussion between the management and the Coordinating Committee.

7.3 Where persons fail to comply with this requirement, measures shall be taken accordingly at the national level pursuant to national legislation and the rules pertaining to employment contracts in force in the country concerned.

7.4 Akzo Nobel N.V. is entitled to refrain from communicating any information to the Forum, the Coordinating Committee or the delegates which, according to objective criteria, might damage the interests of Akzo Nobel N.V. and/or one of the other companies in the Akzo Nobel group or which might constitute infringement of stock market rules or of other provisions.

§8 – EXPERTS

8.1 The Forum shall be entitled to call in experts inasmuch as this is necessary for it to perform its duties in an appropriate manner. The Forum shall endeavour to use the internal expertise of Akzo Nobel N.V. as far as possible.

8.2 The appropriate costs (the usual costs for the type of consultancy concerned) of one external expert per item of the agendas of the joint meetings shall be covered by Akzo Nobel N.V. after agreement has been reached accordingly with the management.

8.3 Where the Forum considers it necessary for the agreed expert to be present for a given agenda item, that expert may, with management approval, be invited by the Forum to take part in the joint meeting and to advise the Forum. Within the context of that advisory role, the expert shall be entitled to call on the management representatives present at the meeting to clarify any questions relating to the agenda item for which the expert has been called in which are still open.

8.2 All experts shall undertake by means of an agreement to be concluded beforehand in writing to refrain from disclosing any confidential information which is made available to them.

§9 – FINANCING

9.1 The (appropriate) costs in the due performance of the duties of the Forum shall be borne by Akzo Nobel N.V. or its subsidiaries. The costs shall include travel and accommodation expenses as well as expenditure for the time spent on activities connected with the Forum and/or the Coordinating Committee.

9.2 The delegates shall be released from their normal activities with continued payment of their salaries and relevant bonuses in order to participate in the meetings of the Forum and/or the Coordinating Committee; this time release shall also apply to traveling time.

9.7 The delegates shall be provided with appropriate means by their respective undertakings for preparing properly for the meetings of the Forum and Coordinating Committee and for the ordinary meetings which they attend and for subsequently informing the relevant employees in accordance with Point 6.8, making extensive use of the available procedures and communication facilities.

§10 – PROTECTION

10.1 The delegates shall enjoy the same protection and guarantees with respect to their duties as apply to the employee representatives in the country in which they are employed.

10.2 In particular, employees in their capacity as delegates must not be dismissed because of activities they have duly carried out for the Forum – irrespective of the existence of legally established protection rights in the country concerned.

§11 – TERM

11.1 The present agreement shall enter in effect on 1 January 1997 and shall end after a term of four years on 31 December 2000.

11.2 Unless, from the point of view of both parties, there is an obvious need for immediate change in order to ensure performance of the agreement, the Coordinating Committee and the management shall, in a spirit of cooperation, jointly review how the agreement has been working after a period of three years. The participation of the individual countries shall also be a subject of this review.

Should the management or the Forum decide by a two-thirds majority to renew an amended version of the agreement beyond 1 January, the Coordinating Committee and the management shall endeavour to present proposals for amendment on the occasion of the joint meeting with a view to reaching an agreement by 1 January 2001. Adequate time shall be planned for these negotiations in addition to the regular course of proceedings at the joint meeting concerned.

Where it proves impossible to reach agreement in good time, the present agreement shall remain in effect until either agreement is reached on the new agreement or the agreement in effect is terminated by one of the parties in writing subject to six months' notice.

Amendments and additions to the present agreement shall require the approval of a two-thirds majority of the delegates.

§12 – COURT OF JURISDICTION

12.1 The present agreement shall be governed by the laws of the Netherlands. Where it is translated into other languages the English version shall be the authoritative version.
12.2 In the event of any dispute arising from the agreement which cannot be resolved despite the efforts of both parties to reach a solution in a spirit of cooperation, the chamber of the Amsterdam Court of Appeal competent for corporate law shall adjudicate the issue with the exception matters falling within the jurisdiction of other courts in the Netherlands or abroad, including supranational courts.

Signed on 20 February 1997
Akzo Nobel N.V.
Employees representatives

Annex 1

This side document is created to clarify clause 9.5 of the EWC Agreement 2013.

9.5 Each (candidate) Delegate will be continuously provided with such English proficiency training as is appropriate to enable that (candidate) Delegate to put himself towards a candidate for election on the EWC AN and enable that (candidate) Delegate to properly perform its duties on the EWC AN.

In order to get substance to what has been agreed with the European Works Council on the English proficiency training, please find below the explanation.
LEVEL OF ENGLISH

- First step is an assessment of English proficiency preferably by Berlitz.
- Berlitz level 7 or 8 should be reached.
- Together with the training company a plan should be set up so that level 6 can be reached within 1-year maximum. Level 718 should be the ambition.

HOW TO TRAIN

- Means of training is preferably face to face training – if necessary in ‘crash courses’ of several days I weeks.
- Training (and travel to and from if needed) takes place within working hours.
- After having reached Berlitz level 8 ‘fresh – up I keep level’ training is provided if necessary.

REFRESHER TRAINING

- To ensure continuous English proficiency training, we will invest in refresher training before the Spring and Autumn Main Meeting for all non-native EWC Delegates.

- This refreshment training will be done centrally, at the venue where the meeting takes place.
- To make this happen we will ask the Delegates to be available in the morning of the first day of the meeting.
- For some Delegates, this will imply that they need to fly in the day before. If this is necessary, Management is committed to make this happen and will allow Delegates to fly in the day before.
- Training is provided in groups with a maximum size of 6.
- 4 hours of training are provided (for example 9- 13 hours).

ORGANIZATION AND COSTS

- Both the National Coordinator as well as the manager are responsible that English Training is provided according to the agreement.
- Training (and travel to and from if needed) takes place within working hours.
- The costs of the language training go to AkzoNobel and will be beard by the cost account of the department of the Delegate.
- Only the costs of the refresher training on the spot of the EWC Main meeting will be beard by Headquarters.
- In case of problems the Counsel for the EWC can be asked for help and will see to the fact that training is provided according to the agreement.

e. TNT – renegotiated agreement 2011

TNT Express – European Works Council / May 2011

The undersigned:

1. TNT N.V., with its registered office in Hoofddorp, the Netherlands, represented by (i) Mrs. M.-C. M. Lombard and (ii) Mr. B.L. Bot;
2. TNT Express N.V., with its registered office in Hoofddorp, the Netherlands, represented by (i) Mrs. M.-C. M. Lombard, Chief Executive Officer, (ii) Mr. B.L. Bot, Chief Financial Officer and (iii) Mr. S. Scheers, Managing Director Group Human Resources;
   and
3. The TNT N.V. European Works Council, represented by Mr. C.M. Degeling, as its Chairman and Mrs. D. Vymazal as its Vice Chairman, Mrs. V. van Wijngaerden as its Secretary and Mr. F. Wip (EWC);

Whereas:

(A) The TNT European Works Council (EWC) was established by an agreement signed on 16 November 2000, as renewed on 5 February 2009;
(B) TNT N.V. intends to demerge the Express activities from TNT N.V., creating two stand-alone groups (Demerger);
(C) The parties have agreed in the process of the Request for Opinion on the split of TNT to conclude this agreement in full conformity with the recast EC Directive 2009/38 EC including its intentions, principles, definitions and clauses;
(D) In the consultation and information phase on the Demerger, both the EWC and TNT N.V.'s management have discussed the changes that were required in light of the Demerger, taking into account article 7.2 of the 2009 EWC agreement (Consultation);
(E) In the Consultation, parties have agreed to amend the current EWC agreement by creating a separate EWC Mail and Express agreement, under the new recast EC Directive 2009/38/EC and by including certain additional elements[142]
(F) In anticipation of this agreement coming into effect, new Members of the EWC will be elected to represent those countries where TNT Express has employees, but where the number of employee representatives in the TNT N.V. EWC is below the number that this country would be entitled to under the art. 4.1 of this agreement. These members will have an observer role until such time that this agreement comes into effect;
(G) This agreement will be entered into between TNT N.V. and the EWC of TNT N.V. The executive management of the TNT Express organisation will acknowledge this agreement by co-signing;
(H) Pursuant to these amendments, this agreement will (i) come into effect between TNT Express N.V. and the EWC Express as of the Demerger and be conditional

142. Request for Opinion of 19 October 2010, Opinion of 26 November of 2010 and Response to EWC Opinion of 1 December 2010.

on the Demerger, (ii) replace the 2009 EWC agreement between TNT N.V. and the EWC and (iii) apply to the TNT Express group, which will be controlled by TNT Express N.V. as per the Demerger. The existing EWC of TNT N.V. will dissolve as a result of this agreement coming into force. Upon entering into force, this agreement shall have a duration of 4 years as per date of it entering into force.

Declare to have agreed as follows:

I. General

Article 1. Guiding Principles

Objective

The objective of the 'TNT Express' European Works Council Agreement (the Agreement) is to establish an EWC for the purpose of implementing the right of 'TNT Express' employees to information and consultation within the geographical scope of this Agreement as laid down in article 3 of this Agreement.

Spirit

Management representatives as well as employee representatives shall co-operate in a spirit of good faith and mutual trust. They shall have due regard to their reciprocal rights and obligations as well as due consideration for the interests of 'TNT Express' as a whole.

Legislation

TNT Express N.V. headquarters in Hoofddorp, the Netherlands, (Management Representatives) shall take on the obligations under Directive 2009/38/EC as central management, and the latest applicable Dutch European Works Council Act shall govern the present Agreement.

Article 2. Definitions

a) *The European Works Council* (EWC): is a body composed of 'TNT Express' employees representing the employees of the companies belonging to the group of companies consisting of TNT Express N.V. as the controlling entity (in the meaning of article 2 of the Dutch Act on the European Works Councils) insofar as the activities of these companies are carried out within the geographical scope of this Agreement).
b) *Information*: transmission of data by the employer to the employees' representatives in order to enable them to acquaint themselves on the subject matter and to examine it. Information shall be given at such time, in such fashion and with such content as are appropriate to enable employees' representatives to undertake an in-depth assessment of the possible impact and, where appropriate, prepare for consultations with the competent organ of 'TNT Express'.
c) *Consultation*: the establishment of dialogue and exchange of views between employees' representatives and central management or any more appropriate

level of management, at such time, in such fashion and with such content as enables employees' representatives to express an opinion on the basis of the information provided about the proposed measures concerning to which the consultation is related, without prejudice to the responsibilities of the management, and within a reasonable time, which may be taken into account within TNT Express. The consultation shall be conducted in such a way that the employees' representatives can meet with the central management and obtain a response, and the reasons for that response, to any opinion they might express.

d) *Companies*: are all companies who are controlled by TNT Express N.V., according to the legislation governing this Agreement.

e) *Members of the EWC*: employees of the companies, duly (s)elected as representatives of 'TNT Express' employees within the geographical scope of this Agreement;

g) *Plenary meeting*: meeting between the EWC and Management Representatives.

Article 3. Scope

This Agreement covers the entire 'TNT Express' workforce in all its companies, whatever their size, in all countries within the European Economic Area. This Agreement also applies for Switzerland. The EWC shall be competent for information and consultation on issues which are of importance for the TNT Express companies within the geographical scope of this Agreement as a whole or TNT Express companies in at least two different states within the geographical scope of this Agreement.

The management and members of the EWC will discuss matters of a strategic and general character concerning TNT Express as a whole at transnational level, as laid down in Article 5 of this Agreement. The EWC will not involve itself in matters which concern no or only one state within the geographical scope of this Agreement.

II. Composition of the European Works Council

Article 4.1 Composition of the EWC

The EWC shall comprise of employee representatives selected under the procedure referred to under Articles 4.1 to 4.4.

The EWC shall consist of one member for each country that employs 20 or more persons within the geographical scope of this Agreement in which 'TNT Express' employees are employed and one, two or three supplementary members, respectively, for each country within the geographical scope of this Agreement in which at least 3,000, 8,000 or 15,000 employees, respectively, of 'TNT Express' are employed. At the time of its institution pursuant to this Agreement, the EWC shall thus be composed of 31 members.

In summary, countries will have members according to the following distribution key:

20–3,000 employees:	1 representative
3,001–8,000 employees:	2 representatives
8,001–15,000 employees:	3 representatives
15,001–	4 representatives

The maximum number of seats a country can obtain on the EWC is four. If the total number of employees within the geographical scope of this agreement increases or decreases with 20% or more, management and the Select Committee will enter into discussion to adapt the distribution key.

The EWC shall, however, not have more than 35 members. The Select Committee, as mentioned under article 4.5, and Management Representatives can decide to allow for more than 35 members for a restricted period in case of acquisitions or in case the number of countries in the European Union will increase. For each member, one substitute member from the same country will be designated in accordance with the laws and practices in the relevant state within the geographical scope of this Agreement. The substitute member may only attend a regular or extraordinary EWC meeting to replace the regular EWC member, if this member is unable to attend. In that case, resources allocated to the regular EWC member shall be shared with the substitute member. There will be no separate facilities for the substitute members. Facilities can be given on an ad hoc base, to be decided by the Select Committee and Management Representatives. Article 6.1 of this Agreement on protection is applicable.

The EWC in consultation with management will ensure that another EWC member will be deemed to represent employees of countries with less than 20 employees.

Article 4.2 Selection of Members of the EWC

The process for electing individual members of the EWC and the procedure for renewal will be in accordance with the laws and practices in each state within the geographic scope of this Agreement. Where appropriate, members of the EWC shall, if feasible, be selected from as many different 'TNT Express' activities as is possible, but only if the headcount in an individual country justifies the appointment of more than one member of the EWC.

All parties will take into account, where possible, the need for balanced representation of employees with regard to their activities, category of worker and gender in the composition of the EWC, without prejudice to national law and custom.

Article 4.3 Eligibility

The Members of the EWC and their substitutes must be employees, as defined by the laws and practices in their country of employment, of one of the 'TNT Express' companies within the geographic scope of this Agreement, and normally must have at least 12 months' company service.

Article 4.4 Term of Office

In the event of an EWC member leaving 'TNT Express' or resigning from the EWC, a new member shall be appointed following the rules outlined above, unless the laws and practices in the relevant state within the geographical scope of this Agreement provide for the substitute member to replace him for the remaining period of the term for which the EWC member was elected.

The Members of the EWC and their substitutes, other than those members elected a new for the first term of this Agreement, will be elected for a renewable period of four (4) years. If, however, a new member has to be appointed in the situation referred to above, this member shall be elected for the remaining period of the term of four years for which the member was elected who left 'TNT Express' or resigned from the EWC.

Transition clause:

The term of office of employees being an EWC member immediately prior to the Demerger will not change as a result of this Agreement. Consequently, the term spent as a member of the EWC under the 2009 agreement will be counted in. The term of office of members elected a new for the first term of this Agreement shall not exceed the term of the current members.

Article 4.5 Select Committee

The EWC shall elect a Chairman and a Secretary. The EWC shall select a Select Committee composed of the Chairman, the Secretary and three additional members. No state within the geographical scope of this Agreement can have more than two members in the Select Committee. The members of the Select Committee will be elected for a renewable period of four (4) years, taking into account the transition clause under article 4.4 which applies mutatis mutandis to the members of the Select Committee.

The Select Committee has the right to meet twice per year to prepare the regular EWC meetings and twice for other reasons. More meetings will be discussed and decided by the Select Committee and Management Representatives.

III. Functioning of the European Works Council

Article 5.1 Regular Meetings

There will be two (2) regular meetings of the EWC with Management Representatives per year. The meetings have a normal duration of two days. The first regular meeting of the year will normally be held around the month of April and the second in the autumn. The members of the EWC should have the opportunity to arrive the day previous to the meeting and return home at the end of the second day.

The first meeting of the year will take place in the Netherlands. During the plenary meeting the CEO of TNT Express N.V. will be present and the Managing Director Group Human Resources will chair the meeting.

The second meeting will take place in one of the other involved countries to be decided by the Select Committee and Management Representatives. The involved country manager will host the meeting. The chairman of the EWC will chair the second meeting. The Managing Director Group Human Resources and, if necessary, a member of the Board will be present.

Management Representatives, chosen for their expertise, may take part m the meetings to provide appropriate information.

The extraordinary meetings may take place in one of the other countries, to be decided by the Select Committee and Management Representatives.

The EWC or the Select Committee has the right to hold a preparatory meeting among themselves, prior to the regular or extraordinary meetings with Management Representatives. The EWC or the Select Committee may also meet immediately afterwards to evaluate the meeting with Management Representatives.

Article 5.2 Content Regular Meetings

The content of the regular meetings and the purpose of the information and consultation will be an exchange of views and dialogue on the basis of a written report drawn up by Management Representatives on the development of the activities and the prospects of the 'TNT Express' activities within the geographical scope of this Agreement. The information and consultation shall in particular focus on the following issues: the structure of the 'TNT Express' group of companies within the geographical scope of this Agreement, its economic and financial situation, probable changes in the relevant activities, production and sales, investments, substantial changes in the organisation, the introduction of new working methods or production processes, environmental care, mergers, relocations, staff reductions or closures of companies, the current employment situation and trends therein and collective redundancies, cross-border HRM policies, in the area of health and safety issues, working time and equal opportunities, provided that these issues are of importance for 'TNT Express' companies in at least two different states within the geographical scope of this Agreement. The written report shall include social information and business plans.

Issues as collective labour agreements, compensation, salaries or benefits, and individual matters which are principally related to only one state within the geographical scope of this Agreement will continue to be handled locally in accordance with the laws and practices in the relevant state within the geographical scope of this Agreement.

Article 5.3 Special Circumstances

Management Representatives shall inform the EWC or the Select Committee as soon as possible concerning special circumstances and proposed decisions which have significant consequences for the interests of the employees of at least two 'TNT Express' companies in two different states within the geographical scope of this Agreement, in particular pertaining to the relocation or closure of companies, or collective redundancies. If the EWC or the Select Committee so requests, it may meet with Management Representatives or a more appropriate management level within 'TNT Express' which has its own powers of decision with respect to the issues to be dealt with, in order to be informed and consulted in more detail on the basis of a written report drawn up by Management Representatives. This extraordinary meeting shall take place at such a time that the information and consultation is still meaningful. The EWC or Select Committee may issue an opinion on the report after the meeting has ended or within a reasonable period after the meeting. Management Representatives and Select Committee will agree on a time frame on a case by case basis.

Consultation will take place with the intention to reach mutual understanding. If it concerns a meeting with the Select Committee, the members of the EWC elected by the employees of the companies directly affected by the measures shall also be invited to attend. The meeting shall not affect the prerogatives of Management Representatives.

The Select Committee and Management Representatives have to decide if there are special circumstances that justify an extraordinary meeting.

Article 5.4 European and National Processes

Information and consultation in the EWC will not replace any information and consultation rights at local or national level. Where there are transnational issues that also call for both information and consultation at national or local level in any country within the geographical scope of this agreement, parties shall endeavour to ensure that the information and consultation process at European level and national level shall begin in a coordinated manner. Where possible, all levels will be informed at an early stage, allowing for enough time for consultation to have a meaningful effect. A more detailed time schedule allowing for the coordination of information and consultation processes will, if necessary, be agreed between the Management Representatives and the SC, with the additional participation of all countries directly involved, whereby at least:

- The European-level information and consultation will follow the procedures set out in this agreement.
- National-level information and consultation will follow the processes required by national law and/or practice. The foregoing does not affect or expand the rights of national consultative bodies and only applies if such a body has both an information and consultation right on the subject matter at hand.

Article 5.5 Select Committee and Management Representatives

The select committee will receive from the Management Representatives a quarterly financial update including explanation by senior management.

A team consisting of two Management Representatives and the Select Committee members shall deal with:

1. setting the precise date and location of the meetings;
2. the agenda of the meetings;
3. reviewing the draft minutes of the meetings as prepared by Management Representatives, including preparing an action list, if any;
4. translations and simultaneous interpretation facilities;
5. co-ordinating training and the use of experts;
6. trying to dissolve any disagreement on the interpretation and/or execution of this Agreement;

7. interpretation facilities and the administrative facilities mentioned in article 5.13;
8. setting up working groups from among the Members of the EWC. Such working groups may only call in the assistance of experts if and to the extent that an annual budget has been agreed upon between the parties as per article 6.2.

Article 5.6 Agenda

The Select Committee and Management Representatives are responsible for calling the meetings by sending written invitations, the agenda and accompanying documentation, if any, at such a time that the members of the EWC or its Select Committee have time to prepare themselves for the meetings. In respect of the regular meetings, the agenda and accompanying documentation, if any, will be sent in principle four weeks before the date of the meeting between the EWC and Management Representatives. In case no relevant information is available two weeks before the EWC meeting, the Select Committee and Management Representatives will decide whether it is relevant to continue with the agenda point concerned.

The Select Committee and Management Representatives convene not later than six weeks before the regular meetings to be able to take care of the appropriate preparations for the meetings.

Article 5.7 Experts

The EWC may be assisted by one (1) permanent expert insofar as this is necessary for the accomplishment of its tasks. Additional experts can be hired after discussion and mutual agreement between the Select Committee and Management Representatives. Experts should be willing to sign a non-disclosure agreement regarding confidential information. Experts may be required to confirm in writing that they do not assist competitors of 'TNT Express'.

Article 5.8 Languages

The EWC and management plenary meeting shall be held in English. The agenda, minutes and any additional information mentioned on the agenda shall be produced in English and translated into other official EU languages on request. To ensure as far as possible that there is meaningful exchange of views, simultaneous interpretation facilities shall be made available on request.

Article 5.9 Dissemination of Information

Without prejudice to obligations of confidentiality imposed on the Members of the EWC, the EWC may communicate the information received to the respective country representative bodies as well as through using the EWC website and existing 'TNT Express' magazines. In countries where there is no representative body, the member of the EWC of this country may, in accordance with local laws and practices and with the exception of confidential information, communicate the information received to the employees of his country.

Article 5.10 Confidentiality

The meetings of the EWC will be deemed 'open', unless a topic is identified as confidential by Management Representatives.

In principle 'TNT Express' management will provide the EWC with information it deems confidential. All Members of the EWC shall be bound to respect the confidentiality of information and agree not to disclose confidential information at any time, including after the end of their mandate. Any involved experts shall sign a specific agreement to respect confidentiality. Management Representatives may ask the Members of the EWC to sign a confidentiality agreement in circumstances where Management Representatives themselves have signed such a confidentiality agreement.

Management Representatives will indicate the grounds for imposing confidentiality before the information is provided and how long confidentiality will last as well with whom the information can be shared. Management Representatives shall not unreasonably designate information as confidential.

Any breach of confidentiality obligations by an EWC member may lead to legal and/or disciplinary action in accordance with the 'TNT Express' Business principles and 'TNT Express' Group Policy on Disciplinary Actions. In case of a breach of confidentiality, the Chairman of the EWC will be informed.

Article 5.11 Withholding of Information

'TNT Express' is not obliged to provide information as far as this would violate mandatory regulations or seriously prejudice or harm its legitimate interests.

Article 5.12 Training

It is the intention of 'TNT Express' that the members of the EWC are properly trained to take an effective part in the EWC and plenary meetings, and necessary, relevant, preferably joint, training will be provided. During the four years' period a minimum of 4 days training will be available. If needed also individual English languages trainings can be provided. Requests for training will be co-ordinated by the Select Committee and Management Representatives. For practical reasons the training will, as far as possible, be combined with the regular meetings.

Article 5.13 Facilities

The members of the EWC receive reasonable (communication) facilities to carry out their duties and responsibilities as member of the EWC. The members of the EWC have the right to communicate with employees or their representatives in other companies in their country. Local management will be informed about these facilities.

Travel and accommodation costs shall be dealt with in accordance with prevailing business travel rules determined by 'TNT Express' and borne by 'TNT Express'.

The EWC will receive necessary administrative support.

'TNT Express' shall bear the costs for preparatory meetings of the EWC or its Select Committee, experts (provided that the costs do not exceed the budget), the regular meetings, extraordinary meetings, interpretation and translation, and training. The parties to this Agreement agree that the EWC should operate in the most cost-effective and efficient manner and shall where possible limit the need for interpreters and translators and ensure that EWC meetings are conducted in a timely and efficient manner. The expenses reasonably necessary for the European Works Council and the select committee to exercise their functions shall be borne by TNT Express.

IV. Various Items

Article 6.1 Protection of Members of the EWC

The Members of the EWC and their substitutes enjoy the employment protection in accordance with the laws and practices in force in their country of employment.

'TNT Express' management shall ensure that the Members of the EWC and their substitutes will be protected from dismissal or suffer other negative effects on their professional careers with 'TNT Express' or on the workplace as a result of their activities for the EWC.

Article 6.2 Budget

Select Committee and Management Representatives may agree to an annual budget for the EWC. This budget, if agreed upon, shall decide on the maximum level of costs to be incurred by the EWC for the relevant budget year in relation to:

- facilities and costs provided for in accordance with article 5.13;
- experts called in by the EWC, in accordance with article 5.7;
- training for Members of the EWC as provided for in accordance with article 5.12.

If the parties have agreed to such a budget, 'TNT Express' shall only be required to bear the costs exceeding this budget if 'TNT Express' has agreed prior to making the costs exceeding the budget. In case of major events, not covered under the normal consultation articles, the Select Committee and Management Representatives will discuss the height of the possible occurring costs.

Article 6.3 EWC Regulation

Each EWC member has one vote. Decisions of the EWC require a majority.

The EWC may draw up internal regulations, providing for rules of procedure for the EWC and the Select Committee. Prior to its adoption, Management Representatives shall be given the opportunity to make its standpoint known and the EWC and Management Representatives shall try to agree on the contents. These internal EWC regulations may not be contrary to the contents of this Agreement and shall be binding for the members of the EWC only.

V. Final Provisions

Article 7.1 Applicable Law

This Agreement shall be governed by and *interpreted* in accordance with Dutch law.

In the event of differences of opinion regarding the interpretation and/or application of this Agreement, the parties shall make a best effort to settle such differences of opinion amicably and/ or via mediation. If the parties are not successful, the remaining dispute shall be dealt with in the Netherlands according to the procedures laid down in the Dutch European Works Council Act. The dispute can be brought by either party before the Enterprise Chamber of the Court of Appeal of Amsterdam, the Netherlands. The parties agree that this court has exclusive jurisdiction over such disputes.

Article 7.2 Commencement and Duration of the Agreement

This Agreement is conditional upon the completion of the Demerger. This Agreement commences on the date of Demerger and is entered into for a definite period of time of four years. The 2009 EWC agreement shall lapse as per the date of commencement of this Agreement.

At the end of the fourth year Management Representatives and the EWC will evaluate this Agreement. On the basis of this evaluation a renewal for the same period or a renegotiation will take place. In the case of such renegotiation, this Agreement shall remain valid until a new agreement has entered into force.

Article 7.3 Adaptation

This Agreement may be amended by mutual written agreement between the parties, without either party being obliged to enter into renegotiations about proposed changes by the other party, during the duration of this Agreement.

However, both parties agree to amend the Agreement in the following circumstances:

(a) a significant change to TNT Express or the TNT Express group, for example due to a merger, acquisition or division;
(b) a significant change to the workforce of the TNT Express group, insofar as a change in seat allocation, as described below, or distribution key as set out in article 4.1, would insufficiently reflect the new situation. Each year the EWC will be informed of changes to the overall number of companies within the geographical scope of this Agreement.

If TNT Express acquires a company within the geographical scope of this Agreement, the following applies:

- the existing Member(s) of the EWC from the country concerned will also be considered to represent the employees of the newly acquired company, until the next term of office unless the Select Committee and Management Representatives jointly decide otherwise;
- if the acquisitions results in another allocation of seats, as set out in article 4.1,

  (i) extra seat(s) will be given during the term of office to the country or countries that have the right to more member(s) in the EWC provided that the maximum of 35 members is not exceeded; and

(ii) a balanced representation of the companies in the country where the acquisition took place, including the acquired company, will be taken into account for the new allocation of seats, without prejudice to national law;

- if the country in which the acquisition take place is not yet represented in the EWC and this company employs more than 20 employees in that country, the parties concerned shall use reasonable efforts to ensure elections or, as appropriate, selections of new Members of the EWC are initiated within a reasonable period after completion of the acquisition, but in any case within one (1) year thereof;
- If the newly acquired company has established its own European works council, the Management Representative will, following the acquisition, initiate discussions with (the select committees) of both EWCs on the integration of both European works councils.

If TNT Express demerges a part of its group, which fulfils the criteria of a Community-scale undertaking or group under the Directive, and no third party becomes or is expected to become the controlling undertaking in the meaning of article 3 of the Directive, TNT Express underscores the principle that the demerged part will have a European works council based upon materially the same terms as this Agreement.

If TNT Express disposes a company within the geographical scope of this Agreement, resulting in a change of seat allocation, such a change will take place as per the date of the disposal.

In the event Directive 2009/38/EC has been revised, Management Representatives and Select Committee will discuss the impact and decide if realignment of this agreement is necessary.

Article 7.4 Language

In the event of differences of interpretation, the English text of this Agreement prevails.

Article 7.5 Binding Text

The English text is the only binding text.

Article 7.6 Transfer of Rights and Obligations

The members of the EWC of TNT N.V. formally acknowledge that at the date of its first meeting after the Demerger, the Express EWC shall assume all applicable rights and obligations exercised by the EWC of TNT N.V. The EWC of TNT N.V. shall automatically dissolve as per the date of the Demerger.

The rights of the EWC of TNT N.V. in relation to the 'Working' Agreements concerning TNT Group policies, as agreed September 15, 2009 for the EWC of TNT N.V. and the arrangements involving the EWC in the 'Code of Conduct on Responsible Restructuring' will be transferred to the EWC of TNT Express.

As per the Demerger TNT Express N.V. shall assume all rights and obligations of TNT N.V. under this Agreement. As per the Demerger the EWC agreement between TNT N.V. and the EWC shall terminate and this Agreement shall only exist between TNT Express N.V. and EWC Express.

The entire agreement between the parties with respect to the subject-matter herein is contained in this Agreement and shall be governed by the terms and conditions set forth in this Agreement. This Agreement supersedes all previous agreements oral or written between the parties with respect to the subject matter herein.

VI. Date and Signatures

This Agreement is entered upon on May 2011 in Hoofddorp, the Netherlands.
(Signed by management and employee representatives).

f. Akzo Nobel – renegotiated agreement 2012

AkzoNobel Group – European Works Council / October 2012

AMENDED AND RESTATED AGREEMENT ON THE EUROPEAN WORKS COUNCIL AKZONOBEL

The Undersigned

1. Representatives of the employees of the AkzoNobel Group (as defined hereafter) in the Territory (as defined hereafter),
   and
2. AkzoNobel N.V., a public company with limited liability, with corporate seat in Amsterdam, The Netherlands ('AkzoNobel'),
   the representatives under 1. above jointly, and AkzoNobel, are each considered a party to this Agreement.

PREAMBLE

A. The European Works Council AkzoNobel (the 'EWC AN') is an organizational structure put in place to improve the right to information and consultation of AkzoNobel employees in the European Economic Area and Switzerland. It has the prime objective to give a wider understanding of the strategies and developments in the AkzoNobel Group, giving the EWC AN the opportunity to express its views on these developments for Management (as defined hereafter) to consider.
B. This Agreement was originally entered into on February 20, 1997. The parties agreed to review the effectiveness and terms of the Agreement every four years. As a result of those reviews, the Agreement was amended and restated on May 25, 2000, April 21, 2004 and March 12, 2009.
C. The parties have recently again reviewed the Agreement, and as a result thereof wish to amend and restate the Agreement as follows:

INTRODUCTORY CLAUSE – DEFINITIONS

'AkzoNobel Group' means all legal entities and partnerships controlled, directly or indirectly, by AkzoNobel N.V. within the Territory. For the purpose hereof control means majority ownership of the shares and/or voting rights of a legal entity or partnership.
'Area' means countries grouped in accordance with Clause 2.4.
'Consultation' means the establishment of dialogue and exchange of views between the EWC AN and Management in accordance with Clause 3.6.
'Select Committee' means the committee of the EWC AN referred to in Clause 2.14.
'Delegate' means a person serving on the EWC AN and elected or appointed in accordance with Clause 2.5.
'Deputy' means a person elected or appointed in accordance with Clause 2.12.

'Directive' means EU Directive 2009/38/EC of 6 May 2009 on the establishment of a European Works Council or a procedure in Community-scale undertakings and Community¬ scale groups of undertakings for the purposes of informing and consulting employees, as amended, supplemented or replaced from time to time.
'EWC AN' means the European Works Council AkzoNobel established pursuant to this Agreement.
'EWC AN Meeting' means a meeting of the Delegates.
'Information' means the information provided by Management to the Select Committee or the EWC AN (as the case may be) in accordance with clause 3.5.
'Joint Meeting' means a meeting of the EWC AN and Management.
'Management' means the person or persons appointed and duly authorized by AkzoNobel to represent the AkzoNobel Group in all contacts with the EWC AN.
'National Coordinator' means the AkzoNobel manager appointed in any relevant country or Area by AkzoNobel to act as liaison between the employees in such country or Area and AkzoNobel for the purpose of the proper implementation of this Agreement.
'Rules of Procedure' means the internal operating rules of the EWC AN as established from time to time by the Delegates.
'Select Committee' means a committee consisting of five members of the EWC AN established in accordance with Clause 2.14, in order to permit coordination and greater effectiveness of the regular activities of the EWC AN.
'Territory' means the Member States of the European Economic Area and Switzerland. Other countries can be added after agreement between the EWC AN and Management.

CLAUSE 1 – EUROPEAN WORKS COUNCIL AKZONOBEL

1.1 By this Agreement the parties establish the EWC AN for the purpose of transnational Information and Consultation of employees of the companies of the AkzoNobel Group within the Territory on the matters listed in Clause 3.2 to the extent those matters concern the AkzoNobel Group as a whole or at least two establishments or companies of the AkzoNobel Group situated in different countries in the Territory.
1.2 This Agreement regulates the cooperation between AkzoNobel represented by Management, and the EWC AN represented by the Delegates.
1.3 This Agreement does not affect the rights and Obligations ensuing from national legislation or other decisions which regulate employee participation in the employer's decision making process, implying that the various national statutory rights and Obligations involving employee participation, which apply to the various AkzoNobel Group companies, remain in full force.
1.4 The EWC AN shall operate in accordance with the Rules of Procedure. Any amendments to the Rules of Procedure, shall be adopted in an EWC AN Meeting. The Rules of Procedure shall at all times comply with the provisions of this Agreement.
1.5 The working language of the EWC AN is English.
1.6 A term of office of the EWC AN is 4 years, starting with the first regular EWC Spring Main Meeting of the year of the renewed agreement.

CLAUSE 2 – CONSTITUTION OF EWC AN AND SELECT COMMITTEE

2.1 The Delegates of the EWC AN collectively represent the interests of employees in the Territory, as described in Clause 1.

2.2 Each country within the Territory, and, to the extent countries are grouped in an Area in accordance with Clause 2.4, each Area, shall be represented by at least one Delegate. If a country or Area has a large number of employees, extra Delegates are added, based on the percentage of the total number of employees in the Territory as set out in the table below.

More than % of total number of employees in the Territory	*Number of Delegates*
0	*1*
5	2
10	3
16.7	4

2.3 The distribution of employees as set out in Clause 2.2 is reviewed once a year by Management and the Select Committee. For the sake of continuity, the number of Delegates per country will be maintained within a term of office unless major changes occur.

2.4 Countries with less than 50 employees can be grouped together to form an Area. All Areas are specified in Schedule 1 to this Agreement. The Select Committee will inform Management of any intended changes to the countries grouped in an Area. The Select Committee and Management will keep Schedule 1 up to date.

2.5 The Delegates shall be elected or appointed by employees or their representatives according to local legislation.

2.6 Each National Coordinator is responsible for either coordinating or organizing an election or appointment of Delegates in his respective country or Area, depending on the arrangements in the country or Area.

2.7 Each Delegate represents the country or Area and not the Business Area, Business Unit or site where he or she works.

2.8 A person can serve as a Delegate only if he or she is employed by a legal entity forming part of the AkzoNobel Group in the Territory. If he or she does no longer meet this requirement he or she must step down as a Delegate.

2.9 Each Delegate must have a reasonable knowledge and command of English. Each (candidate) Delegate has a right to training in accordance with Clause 9.5 of this Agreement.

2.10 Each Delegate is responsible for communicating with the employees of the country or Area, as applicable, in a way according to local customs.

2.11 As a general rule, a Delegate is elected or appointed for a four years' term.

2.12 In each country in the Territory in which one or more Delegates are elected, and in each Area, a Deputy will be appointed or elected in accordance with local legislation. Clauses 2.5 through 2.11 of this Agreement apply equally to Deputies.

Deputies step in temporarily, for the duration of the inability of the relevant Delegate, if:

(a) a Delegate is unable to perform its duties on the EWC AN due to a leave of absence which is likely to exceed six months; or

(b) in a country or Area with only one Delegate, the Delegate is unable to attend an EWC AN Meeting.

A Deputy will permanently replace a Delegate if such Delegate resigns or leaves the company or is expatriated or seconded to a country outside the Territory. In such case, the Deputy will serve the remainder of the term of office of such Delegate, and will be considered a Delegate for the purpose of this Agreement. If the remainder of the term of office is longer than 1 year, counting from the date on which the Deputy has replaced the Delegate, a new Deputy for the relevant country or Area shall be elected.

If a Delegate misses two consecutive EWC AN Meetings, Management and the Select Committee will contact the National Coordinator of that country or Area (as the case may be) to find a solution.

A Delegate may only be replaced by a Deputy for reasons other than specified in this Clause 2.12 or in Clause 2.8 with the approval of the Chair of the EWC AN and of Management. For the sake of effectiveness and continuity of the EWC, any such reasons must be motivated and well founded. Management may withhold its approval at its discretion.

If a Deputy is not available for the purpose of this Clause 2.12, Management and the Select Committee shall agree in good faith on alternative steps, taking into account the continuity of the EWC AN.

2.13 In appointing Management and National Coordinators, AkzoNobel will duly take into account the need for continuity on the part of Management.

2.14 The Delegates will elect a chair, a deputy chair and three Select Committee members that together will make up the Select Committee. The Delegates will also elect two deputy members for the Select Committee. A term of office of the Select Committee will coincide with the term of office of the EWC AN.

2.15 The Select Committee represents the EWC AN between the regular EWC Main Spring and Autumn meetings.

CLAUSE 3 – SUBJECT MATTERS OF INFORMATION AND CONSULTATION

3.1 Within the scope set forth in Clause 1.1, the EWC AN shall be informed and consulted on the development of the activities of the AkzoNobel Group in the Territory.

3.2 Information and Consultation as referred to in Clause 3.1 shall in particular relate to the following items regarding the AkzoNobel Group:

- the structure of the undertaking
- the economic and financial position

- the probable development of the business and of production and sales
- the situation and probable trend of employment
- investment and divestments
- substantial changes concerning organization
- introduction of new working methods or production processes
- reallocation of production
- mergers
- cut-backs or closures of undertakings, establishments or important parts thereof
- collective redundancies
- issues agreed on an ad-hoc basis between Management and the Select Committee as being of interest
- human resources policies
- health, safety and environment policies

3.3 In case of extraordinary circumstances which have a considerable impact on the interests of employees in at least two countries within the Territory, the Select Committee shall be informed in accordance with Clause 5. Extraordinary circumstances are circumstances such as, in the event of relocation, the closure of businesses or establishments, or collective redundancies.

3.4 Management has at no time any Obligation to inform or consult the EWC AN or the Select Committee to the extent it will harm or be prejudicial to the functioning of any company or other entity within the AkzoNobel Group, or is in violation or could contravene stock market rules or other regulatory requirements. Notwithstanding any of its Obligations to inform or consult the EWC AN or the Select Committee under this Agreement, Management has no obligation to inform or consult the EWC AN or the Select Committee prior to informing or consulting local management or local works councils.

3.5 Subject to Clause 3.4, the Information provided should enable the EWC AN to acquaint itself with the subject matter and to examine it. Information shall be given at such time, in such fashion and with such content as is appropriate to enable the EWC AN to undertake an in-depth assessment of the possible impact and, where appropriate, prepare for Consultation without slowing down the decision-making process in the company.

3.6 Subject to Clause 3.4, Consultation shall take place at such time, in such fashion and with such content as enables the EWC AN to express an opinion on the basis of the Information provided about the proposed measures to which the Consultation is related, without prejudice to the responsibilities of AkzoNobel's senior management, within a reasonable time, and which may be taken into account by responsible management.

CLAUSE 4 – REGULAR MEETINGS

4.1 Every year there will be two regular meetings. The spring meeting will be held within four months after the publication of the Annual Report of AkzoNobel. The autumn meeting will be held at an appropriate time.

4.2 The spring and autumn meetings will last two consecutive days each. Each meeting comprises the following sessions:
- an EWC AN Meeting to prepare the Joint Meeting
- a Joint Meeting followed by
- an EWC AN Meeting to evaluate the Joint Meeting.

The autumn meeting should be organized in such a way that it can allow appropriate training for the EWC AN members during the meeting.

4.3 The chair of the Joint Meetings will rotate among Management and the EWC AN Chair.

4.4 At the Joint Meeting the EWC AN will be informed and consulted by Management on the strategies and developments of AkzoNobel. There will be a presentation on the financial situation of AkzoNobel and the strategy of a Business Unit or Business Area. The EWC AN Delegates can make statements and there will be an opportunity to ask questions.

4.5 The Select Committee and Management jointly decide on the agenda of the Joint Meetings. The agenda for the Joint Meeting will be sent to Delegates and National Coordinators.

4.6 A Summary Record of the Joint Meeting will be agreed by the Select Committee and Management at the Meeting. The National Coordinators will translate and distribute the Summary Record to the employees of their countries within four weeks from the day on which the Joint Meeting is held and in accordance with national law and local customs.

4.7 The Select Committee meets at least twice yearly with Management. The Select Committee meetings will be in preparation for the spring and autumn meetings referred to in Clause 4.1. The Select Committee and Management jointly decide on the agenda of the Select Committee meetings. Other Delegates can be invited.

4.8 The Select Committee meeting comprises the following sessions:
- a Select Committee meeting to prepare the Joint Meeting
- followed by a meeting of the Select Committee and Management.

4.9 Management will be responsible for the minutes of the Joint Meeting and the Select Committee and Management meeting. The EWC AN Chair will check the minutes before they are distributed.

4.10 The minutes of the internal meetings will be distributed to the Delegates only. The minutes of the Joint Meetings, and the Select Committee and Management meeting will be distributed to the Delegates and National Coordinators and Management. Minutes will be distributed within eight weeks from the day on which the meeting to which the minutes apply is held.

4.11 An introduction program will be given for new Delegates at the beginning of the new Agreement and when a Delegate joins EWC AN during the term of the Agreement.

4.12 Spring meetings are normally held in Amsterdam. In order to improve the Delegates' understanding of their fellow EWC AN members' working conditions and cultures the autumn meeting shall be held at different AkzoNobel sites within the Territory. Educational site visits and meetings with local employee representatives can be included.

CLAUSE 5 – EXTRAORDINARY CIRCUMSTANCES AND MEETINGS

5.1 In case of extraordinary circumstances referred to in Clause 3.3, an extraordinary meeting between Management and the Select Committee for Information and Consultation purposes will be called. This meeting may take place by means of a telephone conference and shall be held at a time at which such Information or Consultation is still meaningful. Management shall invite other Delegates of countries that may be affected by the extraordinary circumstance, unless this is considered inappropriate by Management, in which case Management will consult with the EWC AN Chair to find a solution.

5.2 At the meeting referred to in Clause 5.1, Management and the Select Committee shall agree on whether a second meeting is appropriate, whether by means of a telephone conference or a physical meeting. The Select Committee and Management will jointly decide on the agenda and the invitees for the meeting.

5.3 During or as soon as reasonably possible after an extraordinary meeting referred to in Clause 5.1 or, if applicable, Clause 5.2, the EWC AN will be given the opportunity to express its opinion regarding the issue in question.

CLAUSE 6 – ORGANIZATIONAL MATTERS

6.1 The EWC AN will be assisted and supported by a Secretariat to be provided by AkzoNobel. The Secretariat will be responsible for organizing all meetings of the EWCAN.

6.2 In each country within the Territory, or, to the extent countries are grouped in an Area, in each Area, a National Coordinator is appointed by AkzoNobel.

6.3 The tasks of the National Coordinator are as follows:
- to arrange that one or more Delegates and Deputies are elected or appointed in accordance with the applicable legislation and/or customs, also taking into account local circumstances and aiming at a fair representation of the employees;
- to see to that the Delegates and Deputies are supplied with relevant means for communication, i.e. computers, telephones and that they get proper training in the use of the equipment etc.;
- to see that the Delegates and Deputies are given enough time in order to fulfil their tasks;
- to provide necessary translations of relevant material and proper distribution of the Summary Record of the Joint Meeting; and
- to support and guide the language training of the Delegates and Deputies.

CLAUSE 7 – CONFIDENTIALITY

7.1 Delegates and Deputies will at no time disclose any information which has been provided to them in confidence.

7.2 Prior to providing information which is of a confidential nature to the EWC AN, the Select Committee or any Delegate or Deputy, Management may require that the relevant Delegates or Deputies on a case-by-case basis confirm that such information shall, until a specified date or until further notice, not be disclosed to any employees or third parties. To allow Delegates to choose not to receive the information, Management shall specify the nature of the information and the reason for its confidentiality. The Select Committee and the Delegates shall not share any such information with any employees or third parties, including trade unions or works councils, until further explicit and express notice from Management.

7.3 Any breach of this obligation will be dealt with at the national level in accordance with national legislation and applicable employment conditions and regulations in the relevant company. In addition, any breach of this obligation may, at the discretion of Management, lead to review of the terms and conditions of this Agreement.

CLAUSE 8 – EXPERTS

8.1 The EWC AN may consult external experts if needed after consultation with Management. The EWC AN shall consider using AkzoNobel's internal expertise as much as possible.

8.2 All experts shall be bound by prior written agreement to keep confidential any confidential information made available to them.

CLAUSE 9 – RESOURCES

9.1 Reasonable costs will be borne by AkzoNobel or any of its subsidiaries. These costs include travel and accommodation costs and expenses incurred for the time spent in connection with the EWC AN and/or the Select Committee. This also includes reasonable costs incurred for communication resources like telephone, fax or access to e-mail or necessary translations.

9.2 Delegates shall be given time-off from their normal duties with continued salary pay and any other applicable allowances, for their participation in the EWC AN and/or the Select Committee meetings, together with the necessary time for traveling and debriefing their constituencies.

9.3 Being a Delegate or a Deputy is a part of regular employment.

9.4 The EWC AN Delegates and their National Coordinator are, in cooperation, responsible for information to the employees in their respective countries.

9.5 Each (candidate) Delegate and Deputy will be continuously provided with such English proficiency training as is appropriate to enable that (candidate) Delegate to put himself forward as a candidate for election on the EWC AN and enable that (candidate) Delegate or Deputy to properly perform its duties on the EWC AN. See annex 1.

9.6 The Select Committee can as agreed with Management be given adequate training to further increase the efficiency and understanding of its tasks.
9.7 The EWC AN will usually have a training day at the autumn meeting to further increase its efficiency and to further the understanding of its tasks.

CLAUSE 10 – PROTECTION

10.1 With regard to their duties, Delegates enjoy the same protection and guarantees provided for employee representatives in the country of employment.
10.2 In particular, irrespective of whether or not national legislation offers any protection in this respect, employees in their capacity as Delegates and Deputies cannot be dismissed on account of work properly carried out for the EWC AN.

CLAUSE 11 – DURATION

11.1 This Agreement is entered into for an indefinite period. A party may terminate this Agreement at any time by giving the other party written notice of termination taking into account a notice period of six months. After having received or having given notice of termination of this Agreement, AkzoNobel will, without delay, start a process for the purpose of the establishment of a European works council or a European employee information and consultation procedure as provided for in the Directive.
11.2 Notwithstanding any apparent need for an immediate amendment, the effectiveness and the terms and conditions of this Agreement will be reviewed by the parties every four years in the underlying spirit of cooperation. For this purpose, the Select Committee and Management will jointly review the Agreement one year prior to the end of each term of office and report on the findings of such a review to the Joint Meeting.
11.3 If agreement on any amendments cannot be reached prior to the expiration of the then current term of office, this Agreement will stay in force, unless a party terminates this Agreement in accordance with Clause 11.1.
11.4 Amendments to this Agreement require the approval of Management and of a two-thirds majority of the Delegates.
11.5 If, following a significant change of the structure of the AkzoNobel Group within the Territory (for example, due to a material merger, acquisition or division), the EWC AN must be adapted in order to properly reflect the new situation and such adaptation cannot be carried out without an amendment of this Agreement, the parties will discuss and negotiate in good faith such amendments to this Agreement as are required reasonably to adapt the EWC AN to the new situation. During these discussions and negotiations and until the necessary amendments have been agreed, the EWC AN will continue to operate in accordance with the terms of this Agreement. The parties hereby express the intent that, in the event that following an acquisition of a company that already has a European works council, there will be another European works council

within the AkzoNobel Group, such other European works council will be dissolved within an agreed timeframe and the EWC AN (to the extent required, as adapted) will be the sole European works council within the AkzoNobel Group. In the event, however, that, notwithstanding the above, both the EWC AN and the other European works council must be dissolved pursuant to Article 13 of the Directive, AkzoNobel will start negotiations for a new agreement as provided in the Directive and will strive to arrive at an agreement on terms that are similar to the terms of this Agreement.

CLAUSE 12 – APPLICABLE LAW

12.1 This Agreement is governed by the laws of The Netherlands. Consequences of changes in governing laws can be included in the Agreement whenever appropriate. Acknowledging that this Agreement may be translated in other languages the parties agree that the English version shall prevail.

12.2 Any disputes arising from this Agreement which, notwithstanding best efforts by both parties to resolve such disputes in the underlying spirit of cooperation, cannot be resolved, will be dealt with by the Enterprise Chamber of the Court of Appeal in Amsterdam with the exception of those matters for which other courts in The Netherlands or abroad, inclusive of any Supranational Courts, will have jurisdiction. AkzoNobel will pay for all costs related to a court case. This also includes specialists called in by the EWC AN.

CLAUSE 13 – ENTIRE AGREEMENT

This Agreement constitutes the entire agreement between the parties with respect to its subject matter and supersedes all prior agreements, representations, writings, negotiations or understandings with respect to that subject matter.

SCHEDULE 1

AREAS

The following countries are grouped together to form an Area:

- Estonia, Latvia and Lithuania
- Spain and Portugal
- Austria, Slovenia and Slovakia
- Belgium and Luxemburg
- Greece and Cyprus
- Bulgaria, Romania and Hungary

ANNEX 1 Language training

Signed on October 25, 2012
Akzo Nobel N.V.

Name: Name:
Representatives of the employees of the AkzoNobel Group, the European Works Council AkzoNobel,
represented by
Chair Deputy Chair
Name: Name:

Annex 1

This side document is created to clarify clause 9.5 of the EWC Agreement 2013.
9.5 Each (candidate) Delegate will be continuously provided with such English proficiency training as is appropriate to enable that (candidate) Delegate to put himself towards a candidate for election on the EWC AN and enable that (candidate) Delegate to properly perform its duties on the EWC AN.

In order to get substance to what has been agreed with the European Works Council on the English proficiency training, please find below the explanation.

LEVEL OF ENGLISH

- First step is an assessment of English proficiency preferably by Berlitz.
- Berlitz level 7 or 8 should be reached.
- Together with the training company a plan should be set up so that level 6 can be reached within 1-year maximum. Level 718 should be the ambition.

HOW TO TRAIN

- Means of training is preferably face to face training – if necessary in 'crash courses' of several days I weeks.
- Training (and travel to and from if needed) takes place within working hours.
- After having reached Berlitz level 8 'fresh – up I keep level' training is provided if necessary.

REFRESHER TRAINING

- To ensure continuous English proficiency training, we will invest in refresher training before the Spring and Autumn Main Meeting for all non-native EWC Delegates.
- This refreshment training will be done centrally, at the venue where the meeting takes place.
- To make this happen we will ask the Delegates to be available in the morning of the first day of the meeting.
- For some Delegates, this will imply that they need to fly in the day before. If this is necessary, Management is committed to make this happen and will allow Delegates to fly in the day before.
- Training is provided in groups with a maximum size of 6.
- 4 hours of training are provided (for example 9- 13 hours).

ORGANIZATION AND COSTS

- Both the National Coordinator as well as the manager are responsible that English Training is provided according to the agreement.
- Training (and travel to and from if needed) takes place within working hours.
- The costs of the language training go to AkzoNobel and will be beard by the cost account of the department of the Delegate.
- Only the costs of the refresher training on the spot of the EWC Main meeting will be beard by Headquarters.
- In case of problems the Counsel for the EWC can be asked for help and will see to the fact that training is provided according to the agreement.

g. Unilever – renegotiated agreement 2014

Unilever – Unilever European Works Council (UEWC) / December 2014

Table of Contents

1. Aim and Status of the Agreement
2. Scope
3. Composition
4. Organisation
5. Competence
6. Confidentiality
7. Duration
8. Interpretation of the Agreement
   Annex 1 Further arrangements regarding Information and Consultation
   Annex 2 Number of UEWC Employee Representatives
   Annex 3 Definitions including Confidentiality definitions
   Annex 4 Consultation protocol

Preamble

- The internationalisation of businesses and the changes in Europe, also in terms of the European Internal Market, are changing the way people think and leading to changes in company structures. In this integration process, which is important for both the company and its employees, economic and social aspects form the basis for a future-oriented company policy.
- In 1996 Unilever formed a European Works Council (UEWC) in order to create a framework for the effective consultation and exchange of information on a European level. Management and employees have now reached a future oriented agreement based on the goodwill and co-operation previously developed. Both management and employees recognise that the framework of the agreement continues to provide a sound basis for consultation. Established practices and further arrangements regarding the implementation of the Information and Consultation process are set out in annex 1
- Many decisions that were once made at national level are now increasingly made interdependently at international levels. Whilst implementation of strategy will be at national/local level by national/local management according to local legislation, the role of the UEWC to consult with management at European level now assumes a greater relevance.
- The development of a fair, frank and trusting relationship between the management, the employees and their operational representatives is important. It will be facilitated by comprehensive and timely communication of information as part of a mutual exchange of views allowing all parties to bring their own ideas into the dialogue. An exchange of information and opinions across the countries will promote mutual understanding and a willingness to co-operate.

- Procedures and definitions which are not mentioned within this agreement, or in the appendices, will be settled on a case-by-case basis in the spirit of trusting co-operation and take account of the rights and obligations of both contracting partners.

1. Aim and Status of the Agreement

The following Agreement under the terms of Article 13 of the AEU Directive (94/45/EC) dated 22nd September 1994 governs supranational information and consultation of employees and their representatives.

2. Scope

This Agreement shall apply to all Unilever companies in the European Economic Area including Switzerland. Companies joining and leaving Unilever NV/PLC in the European Economic Area and Switzerland will be automatically included in the Agreement or respectively excluded from the same. The fact that companies join or leave Unilever PLC/NV shall have no influence on the validity of this agreement.

3. Composition

The UEWC is composed of a management delegation with authority and of an employee delegation. Only employees of Unilever companies that are included within the scope of the UEWC are eligible to be members of the employee's delegation. For the next four years (2014 – 2018) the number of representatives for the respective countries are as stipulated in Annex 2 to this agreement.

Selection or appointment of employee representatives

The employee representatives shall be elected or appointed in accordance with the national legislation collective labour agreements or with current practice.

The employee representatives thus elected or appointed are considered to be fully representative of all Unilever employees in their country including employees who join the Unilever NV/PLC during his/her full term of office.

The term of office of each employee representative in the UEWC shall correspond to his/her national practice but shall normally not be longer than 4 years.

If necessary on business or on personal grounds the succession of an employee representative should be organised in line with the agreed procedure on the selection of employee representatives.

Re-election or re-appointment shall be possible.

The employee members of the UEWC will enjoy the protection that the national legislation and/or practice in their country of employment provides for. By virtue of exercise of their mandate they may neither receive preferential treatment nor may they be disadvantaged; they must receive leave of absence for attending the meetings referred to in this Agreement in accordance with national praxis.

4. Organisation

a) The Management shall appoint an authorised Management Representative.

b) The employee delegation will elect from amongst its members and for its organisation a Chairperson and a Vice-Chairperson.
c) Furthermore the employee delegation in the UEWC may establish a Coordination Committee (the 'ECC') which shall consist of the Chairperson and Vice-Chairperson of the employee delegation and of up to 6 further employee representatives. The tasks of the ECC shall be laid down by the employee delegation in rules and procedures. These rules and procedures shall be submitted to the management for notification. Normally ECC meetings will take place monthly (excepting holiday seasons) but the ECC and management representatives may meet more frequently at the request of the employee or management representatives. The UEWC will elect 3 substitutes for the ECC members from the members of the UEWC in the event that ECC members are unavailable.
d) An ECC Feedback group which shall normally consist of 4 ECC members is tasked with co-ordinating ECC activities and completion of necessary preparation work as required.

   The chairperson convenes the group following an ECC meeting. The effectiveness of this arrangement will be reviewed after 4 years.
e) Twice a year a plenary UEWC meeting shall normally take place in Rotterdam under rotating Chairpersonship of the management and the employee representatives. In the same spirit of this joint body the Chairpersonship of the ECC meetings will also be rotated. One of the 2 UEWC meetings shall be dedicated to training purposes.
f) The employee delegation may hold a preparatory session on the day before the plenary meeting. After the plenary meeting the employee delegation may organise a debriefing meeting. In total the preliminary session plenary meeting and debriefing meeting should not take up more than two days excluding travelling time.
g) The employee delegation shall be entitled in the preliminary session and debriefing meeting as well as in the meetings of the Coordination Committee (art. 4c) to invite internal or external experts of their choice in conjunction with topics which will be dealt with in the UEWC. In so far as this incurs costs which the employee delegation wishes the management to bear prior consent shall be required.
h) It is agreed that all participants shall endeavour to reduce the number of languages used. Representatives elected to the ECC at the time of this agreement can access interpretation or can choose to undertake an intensive language course at the expense of their employing company to enable them to work in English.

   Election onto the ECC is not dependent on the level of knowledge of English however future members are expected to commit to developing their English skills to a level suitable for operating in the ECC. Full language training and translation support will be given, usually for the first 12 months. This arrangement will be reviewed after 4 years.

   All written information prepared by the management as well as the agenda, shall only be drawn up in English. English shall be the authoritative language.

The way information will be disseminated shall be agreed in advance. Translation of all written information, into the respective mother tongue may be undertaken in the respective home country at the expense of the company concerned.

i) The costs connected to the meetings, as well as travelling, accommodation and board for the participants, shall be borne by the company.

5. Competence

a) The subjects of information and consultation shall in particular be the matters listed below being of a cross-border nature and which affect at least two countries within the geographical scope of application of this Agreement:
   - Economic and financial situation
   - Progress of the business in the different sectors
   - Probable trends in employment
   - Investments
   - Significant organisational and structural changes
   - Introduction of new working methods and production procedures
   - Relocation of production and relocation of product lines
   - Workforce reduction in or closure of operational units or major parts thereof as well as collective redundancies.

   By way of example, further themes may be:
   - Health and Safety of employees and Environmental protection
   - Training
   - The situation of women

b) The UEWC shall not infringe the authority and competence of the respective national or local management and the respective national or local employees' representative bodies.

c) Matters relating to employees and companies in just one country shall remain under the exclusive competence of the interlocutors in such country under the rules usual thereto (e.g. matters in conjunction with state legislation or national collective labour agreements; salaries, wages, working conditions, negotiations of any kind; personal or political matters).

d) Tasks of the Chairperson and the Vice-Chairperson of the employee delegation and of the appointed management representative (art. 4a) on behalf of the UEWC Chairperson:
   - Preparation of the agenda for the annual plenary meeting
   - Circulation of the presentations from the UEWC and ECC meetings (subject to confidentiality arrangements).
   - Point of contact between meetings for example in the event of special circumstances significantly affecting employees' interests in several countries. They consult amongst themselves on the necessity and format of all further information and consultation. This could imply the involvement of the Coordination Committee or the respective employee representatives in the UEWC of the countries concerned.

6. Confidentiality

The employee delegation must maintain confidentiality (i.e. based on their national legislation or practices) on all business and company secrets which they learn in their capacity as representatives as well as on all matters designated confidential or whose confidential nature they ought to appreciate in the light of the confidentiality requirement being imposed. This also applies to third party experts.

The duty of confidentiality shall not be terminated by cessation of their representative mandate or by cessation of the involved person's employment at the undertaking.

Management shall not be obliged to provide information which would be prejudicial to the business interests of Unilever.

7. Duration

a) This agreement shall come into force on the day upon which it is signed and shall apply for an indefinite period.
b) Evaluation of this agreement and the functioning of the UEWC under this agreement will take place every 4 years in line with the term of office of the employee representatives. Both management and the employee representatives can make proposals for amendment. If no agreement is reached the existing UEWC agreement will stay valid.
c) In the event of fundamental changes to the EU directive the management and employee representatives can propose amendments to reflect these changes. If no agreement is reached the existing agreement will stay valid.
d) The agreement can be terminated by the majority of the employee representatives or by the European Leadership Team ('ELT') with a notice of one year but not before 4 years have elapsed. Termination can only be justified for exceptional reasons and must be well argued in writing.
e) In case of notice of termination the management and the employee representatives shall evaluate the situation which may lead to a renegotiation of the agreement. If however no agreement is reached before the end of the 1 year of notice period Dutch EWC transposition law will apply.

8. Interpretation of the Agreement

In so far as differences of opinion shall arise between the management and the employee representatives as to the content and interpretation of this agreement, these should be settled within the framework of voluntary negotiations.
Dutch law shall apply.
Rotterdam, December 2014
Herman Soggeberg Jan Zijderveld
UEWC Chairman President Europe
(Followed by signatures of management and employee representatives)

Annex 1

Further arrangements regarding Information and Consultation

a) The body which informs and consults with the UEWC is the European Leadership Team ('ELT'), which is also responsible for the consistency of the process. ELT appoints an authorized Management Representative.
b) Information and Consultation will take place with respect to significant transnational projects.
c) Management recognizes the need to inform on major local issues to the extent they are part of a European strategy and expresses the intention to fulfil this need. For the avoidance of doubt, this intention does not include any Consultation on local issues.

Consultation with the UEWC

d) Any information provided to the UEWC will be adequate and relevant and will be given in good time using cost effective ways of communication.
e) Management recognizes the need to provide the UEWC also with relevant information relating to specific parts of the European Business. All relevant information on specific issues will be made available by ELT via the Management Representative. Appropriate management representation of the European Business will be ensured during the plenary meetings. Employee representatives will inform the Management Representative as early as possible of their information needs in order to facilitate the Information process. As part of an evolutionary process management agrees to continue the dialogue with employees with a view to further improve the information and consultation process regarding the European Business.
f) The need to involve any new EU candidate countries in the future is recognized but prudent timing is important given the state of development of these countries and the more urgent priorities of the Unilever organisations in these countries.

Regarding the role of the plenary UEWC and the ECC:

1) The objective of the plenary UEWC is to be informed and consulted with on relevant transnational issues at a strategic level, including supply chain strategy and the issues mentioned in clause 5. Competence of the agreement. Under normal conditions two plenary meetings will take place per year.
2) The principle role of the ECC, authorized by the UEWC, is to be informed and consulted with on relevant transnational issues on a regular basis.
3) Sufficient time for Information and Consultation will be made available, but always taking into account the complexity of the transnational issue concerned. Without prejudice to the foregoing of this paragraph the start of the

Information and Consultation process will be mutually aligned with any applicable local information and consultation process. The local information and consultation process and the European Information and Consultation process are complementary and are not each other's substitute.

Annex 2

Number of UEWC employee representatives including EWC Chairperson. Country	*Number of Reps.*
Austria	1
Belgium	1
Czech Republic	1
Denmark	1
Estonia	0
Finland	1
France	3
Germany	4
Greece	1
Hungary	2
Ireland	0
Italy	3
Latvia	0
Lithuania	1
Netherlands	3
Norway	0
Poland	3
Portugal	1
Romania	1
Slovakia	0
Spain	2
Sweden	1
Switzerland	2
United Kingdom	4
Grand Total	36

Annex 3

Definitions

Information
The provision of data and the explanations of such data, orally or in writing.

Consultation
Exchange of views and establishment of a dialogue See Annex 4

Employee
All regular staff considered as 'employees' according to the legislation/practice in each Member State of employment.

Unilever company
Any company of which Unilever NV/ PLC or companies belonging to the Concern hold the majority (i.e. 51 %) of the equity.

European Economic Area
The EEA contains the countries as described in the geographical scope of that Treaty.

Management
Management in this agreement refers to the management representatives responsible for the execution of this agreement on behalf of the Central Management.

Employee Delegation
The employee delegation is the group of employee representatives in the UEWC as a whole.

Employee representatives
An employee representative is an employee of a Unilever company elected or appointed as described under Article 3.

Confidentiality
Where documents are marked as:

Embargo: Then no member of the EWC / ECC is permitted to disclose the content of the document to any other person until such time as the embargo is lifted.

Where a document is marked Strictly Confidential ECC Only or EWC only, the document is not permitted to be distributed beyond the EWC / ECC

Where a document is marked as Unilever Internal use only, then whilst the document may be shared with employees for feedback and communication purposes, the document itself cannot be distributed beyond the designated recipients.

Unless a document is not specially marked it is for 'general communication', that means that any documentation received can be distributed to employees or parties external to Unilever without express authorisation.

Within presentations, the confidential information shall be limited to some pages only, so that the remaining presentation is easier to distribute.

Announcement / Decision / Implementation
Announcement shall mean the intention of the European Leadership Team to implement change or take other action, subject to the necessary corporate action and consultation or co-determination procedures in the relevant jurisdictions. An announcement shall not represent the final decision to implement such change or other action.

Decision shall mean that the European Leadership Team has decided to implement in the relevant jurisdictions the change or other action, subject to the necessary corporate action and consultation or co-determination procedures in the relevant jurisdictions.

Implementation takes place when for example, notice of termination is served, production lines are moved or production arrangements are changed or when new organisational structures are enacted.

Transnational
A matter shall be transnational, if it concerns at least two countries within the geographical scope of application of the present Contract. This includes questions regarding one country, as long as they are of importance for the European employees regarding the extent of their possible effects, or if they entail the transfer of activities from one country into another country.

Timely information
Information shall be considered 'timely' if it makes possible a thorough review regarding the consultation, before a final decision is made.

Annex 4

European management and the ECC agreed to adopt the following protocol for the management of consultation at a European level.

To this end there will be two explicit consultation phases:

- Phase 1 – Providing a description of strategic challenges and issues (per category / area etc); this will take place on an ongoing basis with ECC (as per current practice). This phase will become primarily focused on the provision of information to the ECC, on the explanation of issues faced and abstract criteria for cross border decision making, allowing then for the raising and responses to specific questions.
- Phase 2 – This phase will involve consultation on the basis of a proposed decision arising from strategy and cross border decision criteria outlined in phase 1 (typically around a site or selection of sites where restructuring of a transnational nature is proposed).
- Phase 2 consultation will be held at the first ECC meeting after an announcement of a proposed transnational decision in a country, and be completed prior to the implementation of a project. (Subject to the timeline below) The ECC will be formally invited to state their advice either during the ECC meeting or in a reasonable period of time after the meeting. The Company will in all cases advise the ECC of a time period during which it's advice can and will be considered. After the issuing and response to the ECC's advice, then consultation on the issue at a European level will then be completed.

In certain cases, the ECC may choose to issue more than one statement if the consultation of a transnational project is staggered and the business is not able to confirm the number of countries impacted in one meeting.

- In certain cases, where the right conditions exist – dialogue may be held with the ECC during the period when there is not yet a proposed decision, but when alternative directions and possibilities are being explored-at an earlier stage of management deliberation, and prior to any public announcements.

This dialogue held prior to a public announcement will entail:

- Local Reps of any site (s) likely to be under discussion, being advised in advance that dialogue is proposed to begin at a European level to discuss the cross-border aspects of the alternative directions and possibilities.
- Agreement of these Local Reps to this dialogue commencing prior to public announcement (Where local reps object to ECC involvement prior to public announcement – the issue will be referred to the EWC Chairperson for resolution)
- Agreement of ECC and local reps to respect confidentiality during this phase. (It is envisaged that dialogue held at this early stage would be conducted 3 or 4 weeks prior to any possible public announcements).

Where local conditions allow, more public 'review' announcements can be made. In these circumstances, dialogue could be conducted at an even earlier stage of management deliberation. Examples of this have been the 'review' announcements made in the UK. This however requires mutually agreed interpretation of local legal requirements, willingness of all participants to consider all options available, and the operation of a partnership approach to employee relations in the respective countries or locations.

Where Management determines that the conditions above cannot be realized, then Phase 2 consultation on the basis of a proposed decision will commence formally after public announcement. This is understood by all parties as the default position. During the consultation process, both Dialogue or formal process no implementation must take place.

Selected Bibliography

Beurden, P. van (et al.), 2009, Gebruik, niet-gebruik of onderbenutting? Onderzoek naar de mogelijke onderbenutting van bevoegdheden en mogelijkheden door de (Centrale) Ondernemingsraad in grote Nederlandse ondernemingen. Commissioned by the Ministry of Social Affairs and Employment: The Hague.

Bijll Nachenius, H.J. de, 1997, De wet op de Europese Ondernemingsraden, Kluwer: Deventer.

Cremers, J. and Vitols, S., 2016, Takeovers with or without worker voice: workers' rights under the EU Takeover Bids Directive, ETUI: Brussels.

Drongelen, J. van, and S.F.H. Jellinghaus, 2014, Wet op de ondernemingsraden, Paris: Zutphen.

Drongelen, J. van, Fase, W.J.P.M., and S.F.H. Jellinghaus, 2017, Individueel arbeidsrecht: Ontslagrecht, Paris: Zutphen.

Gerlach V. and Broeckhuijsen M.P. van, 2012, De gewijzigde Wet op de Europese Ondernemingsraden: business as usual, ArbeidsRecht 2012/5, Kluwer: Deventer.

Heiden, P. van der (et al.), 2012, Medezeggenschap: Ontwikkelingen in de 21e eeuw, SER: The Hague.

Holtzer, M., 2014, De invloed van werknemers op de strategie van de vennootschap, University of Groningen.

Kaar, R., van het, 2018, Inzicht in de ondernemingsraad, SDU: The Hague.

Kaar, R., van het, E. Smit, W. Buitelaar (et al.), 2006, Vier scenario's voor de toekomst van de medezeggenschap, Eburon: Delft.

Koning, F., 1997, De Europese ondernemingsraad; wet en praktijk, TVVS 1997/3.

Sprengers, L.C.J., 2012, Wet op de Europese Ondernemingsraden, Kluwer: Deventer.

Stoop S. et al., 2011, De Europese ondernemingsraad – Een handboek voor de praktijk, Kluwer: Alphen aan de Rijn.

Verburg, L.G., 2009, 'De herschikking van de EOR-Richtlijn', TRA 2009/43.

Verburg, L.G., 2013, Rood's Wet op de ondernemingsraden, Kluwer: Deventer.

Selected Bibliography

Index

The numbers here refer to paragraph numbers (as enumerated in Parts I and II)

Appropriate level of management, 28–30, 50
Appeal (right of), 4, 62, 106, 115, 122, 141

Co-decision, 10, 11, 116, 129, 131, 133, 143, 145
Community-scale group of undertakings, 17, 22–27
Controlling undertaking, 16, 22–27, 140
Cross-border issues, 28, 30, 49, 88, 89, 112

Decision-making (in an undertaking), 30, 31, 70, 87–90, 118, 129, 142–147

Employee, 18
Employees' representatives, 32–38
  confidentiality, 2, 4, 55, 62, 68–70, 92, 93, 99, 106, 108, 141
  definition, 32, 34, 134
  dismissal protection, 95, 99–106
  facilities, 96–98
  local representatives, 52–55, 67
  merchant seafarer representatives, 36
Employers' associations, 47, 60, 91, 118
Enterprise Chamber of the Amsterdam Court, 4, 62, 106, 115, 121–123, 141
EWC agreements
  absence (in the), 39, 76, 77, 78, 130
  applicability (restructurings), 75, 124
  content, 65, 66, 67–75
  functioning, 49, 81, 126
  negotiations, 48–51, 56
  pre-existing, 109–115
  reference, 65, 76, 77
  renegotiations, 43, 94
  termination, 63, 72, 74, 123
Experts, 2, 58, 59
  confidentiality, 59, 92
  EWC, 84, 91, 92, 126, 130
  SNB, 58, 59, 61

Involved State, 15–20, 34, 37–44, 78, 112, 134

Meetings EWC
  extraordinary, 87, 88, 90, 126
  frequency, 2, 67
  management (with the), 77, 84, 88, 130
  preparatory, 84, 130
Membership
  EWC, 34, 37, 79
  merchant seafarers, 36
  protection, 99, 100, 105
  SNB, 33, 38, 55

Negotiations, 34, 39–43, 48–66, 75–77, 94, 114, 115, 123, 124, 134, 140

Parent undertaking, 17, 22–27, 87

Reasonability
  costs/facilities, 50, 63, 130
  grounds, 69, 141
  time/period, 30

Sanctions, 99, 120, 122
Select committee, 67, 81–84, 87, 90, 91
SNB, 19, 33, 36–38, 42–46
  composition, 33, 36–38, 44–46, 52, 53, 75
  decision-making, 51
  facilities, 50, 58, 95, 96
  legal proceedings, 62, 63
  meetings, 36, 47–53, 61
  nomination, 33, 44, 46, 134
  preparatory meetings, 40

Index

Statute for a European company, 4, 132, 139
Subsidiary requirements, 39, 76–94
  applicability, 48, 57, 77, 115
  provisions, 65
  renegotiation, 94
  select committee, 82

Trade unions, 33, 47, 60, 61, 91, 121

Undertaking from outside the Community, 21

www.ingramcontent.com/pod-product-compliance
Ingram Content Group UK Ltd.
Pitfield, Milton Keynes, MK11 3LW, UK
UKHW020146290926
15471UKWH00004B/717

9 789403 546902